Fired Up

Kindling and Keeping the
Spark in Creative Teams

DR. ANDREW JOHNSTON

Copyright

Published in Nashville, Tennessee through SALT Conferences, a division of Orange Thread Media, LLC.

For bulk, educational or organizational licenses, please contact Orange Thread Media for pricing and details.

Cover Design: Jacob Blaze
Book Layout: Douglas Williams
Edited by: Sara Pack and Luke McElroy

ISBN: 978-0-9913307-2-0
Library of Congress Control Number: 2017957824

Acknowledgements

Thanks to the students who have walked out of my classes to challenge the world. You've shown me how to live better.

Thanks to the leaders who have asked me to walk with them in challenging times. You've shown me what it means to lead better.

Thanks to my wife who has had the challenge of walking with me for a long time. You've shown me what it means to love better.

"Andrew is a seasoned leader, who is as comfortable with C-level executives as he is with new professionals. This book uses a unique blend of humor and insight to tune leaders' perspectives and prepare them for success. *Fired Up* is a practical tool for anyone in management."

JOE SCARLETT
Former, CEO and Chairman, Tractor Supply

"Dr. Andrew Johnston does a masterful job of weaving his decades of experience throughout this work. Readers will want to keep Fired Up readily available on their desk to serve as a strategic reference in leadership and team-building into the future."

DR. CLAUDE PRESSNELL
President, TICUA

"In this book, Dr. Andrew Johnston presents an alternative to the burnout so common in society. He gives you the practical applications and insights to ignite your team's creativity and performance. If you're a leader, you need to read this book!"

ANDREW PINO
VP & General Manager, Salem Church Products

"Quite simply one of the best things I've read recently about doing business in a fractured world."

SUSAN G. WILLIAMS
PhD Professor Emerita of Management,
The Jack C. Massey Graduate School of Business

Contents

Introduction

This book was born in the glow of the fire pit in my backyard. A friend of mine asked me to write a book about leading creatives, and I was mulling it over as I stared into the flames. It was one of those nights when the temperature was perfect for sitting and staring into a fire: cold enough for the heat to be welcome, but warm enough for me to linger.

As I stared into the coals and wondered how I might approach the book, it occurred to me that fire is a fitting metaphor for creativity. Like creativity, it is powerful and mysterious, something we respect and value but do not completely comprehend. The ancient Greeks thought that it was one of four essential elements and that all matter was composed of fire, water, earth, and air. But fire isn't technically an element. It's not even composed of atoms, at least not in the same way as the other three. Fire is actually a reaction, the visible evidence of an invisible communication between matter and energy. That makes it a perfect metaphor for creativity, because creativity involves a comparable translation between the earthly and the ethereal.

When we create, we engage in a process of incarnation that brings our imaginations to life. We use media like words, images, music, light, or movement to translate intangible things like ideas, emotions, and convictions into the physical world we inhabit. To borrow Shakespeare's words from *A Midsummer Night's Dream*, one "gives to airy nothing, a local habitation and a name," and that transformation is as mysterious as fire. Maybe that's why we invoke some of the same imagery in idioms like "igniting creativity," "the spark of ingenuity," or "the fire of genius."

If you lead creatives, the charm and challenge of your role is encouraging that transformation. Your job is to kindle and keep the fire burning in your team, so they can accomplish extraordinary things. This is a tricky proposition. After all, you can't force it to happen or control it directly. That kind of meddling stops the magic and spoils the transformation. Instead, you'll foster the conditions that support it and fan the flames of it when it occurs. This book prepares you to do just that.

When I was in elementary school, a forest ranger came to our class and introduced us to The Fire Triangle. This model presents the three ingredients required for fire to occur: Oxygen, Fuel, and Heat. It reminds you that you will only see flames when you've managed all three well. Similarly, this book prepares you to kindle and keep the fire burning in your creative team, using the wisdom of the fire triangle. It describes the kind of Oxygen, Fuel, and Heat creatives need to burn their brightest.

Oxygen

A fire needs to breathe. Without oxygen, it will sputter, suffocate, and eventually go out. Similarly, the creative flame in your team will flicker and fade unless you give it room to breathe. You fire up creatives when you give them some air and loosen the physical or emotional constraints that hold them back and hem them in. The first section of this book encourages you to prepare their environment, to preserve their margin, and to protect their opportunity to create.

Fuel

A fire also needs to be fed. The powerful transformation that produces light and energy is consuming, and so is the creative process. Your team needs the right fuel to keep it going, or it will quickly burn up or burn out. Kindling and keeping the fire in creatives is often about stoking the fire in their bellies. The second section of this book encourages you to drive out fear, to pump up the purpose, to share the power, to build trust, and to have fun.

Heat

A fire requires heat. Without it, a bonfire is just a pile of sticks. Similarly, if you don't bring the heat, you can pile on all the talent and resources you can find, but you'll never see any flames. Heat ignites the transformation that turns all of that potential into reality. The third section of this book prepares you to turn up the heat by setting ambitious goals, giving effective feedback, and embracing the risks that accompany extraordinary things.

If you manage these three components well, you'll create the conditions that fire up creatives and keep them burning bright. I hope the content of the following pages encourages and equips you to make the most of the men and women you lead. It's not offered as gospel, just good food for thought. These are the kinds of things I would share with you leader-to-leader if we were having a conversation over coffee... or staring into the fire in my backyard.

—

This book prepares you to *kindle and keep* the fire burning in your creative team.

OXYGEN

On a camping trip when I was a kid, I remember being astonished when my father blew our campfire into existence. We had piled some dry leaves and sticks on the grey remains of the previous night's fire, but they just sat there, sad and smoldering, until my father knelt down and blew on them, gently. Suddenly, the coals leaped to life, and bright flames rushed through the pile! Who knew he had such super powers?

I'm older now, and I've worked the same small magic many times myself, but it still astonishes and delights me. With just a few deep breaths, I can resuscitate a lifeless pile of kindling and coals and turn it into a blazing fire. As a leader, you have the same power to kindle a fire in your creatives and see them leap to life.

Fires need oxygen to burn. Without it, they sputter, suffocate, and eventually go out. You can pile on the fuel and turn up the heat, but if you don't give it air, nothing will ignite.

Similarly, if you want to fire up your team, you've got to give them room to breathe. You need to loosen the physical and emotional constraints that hold them back and hem them in. The chapters in this section will help you breathe life into your team by preparing their environment, preserving their margin (and your own), and protecting their opportunity to create.

chapter one

A Highly Oxygenated Environment:

Aligning Context & Culture for Connections, Self-Expression, and Activity

There are two ways of being creative. One can sing and dance. Or one can create an environment in which singers and dancers flourish.

—Warren Bennis

IF YOU'VE EVER been in a highly oxygenated environment, like a laboratory or a hospital room, you've seen the no-smoking signs and the warnings against open flame. All of that oxygen makes for an especially flammable atmosphere, and even the smallest spark could start a blaze.

Metaphorically speaking, that's exactly the kind of situation you want to create if you are trying to kindle and keep the fire burning in your team. Think of yourself as an atmospheric engineer. You're creating an environment that gives creatives room to breathe and urges even the smallest sparks of imagination to burn.

To that end, you need to pay attention to both the physical spaces and the culture of your team.

Physical Spaces

Physical spaces exert a powerful influence on the things that happen in them. I experienced this a couple of years ago when my wife and I attended a sung mass at St. Paul's Cathedral in London. As I sat in the 300-year-old hall, listening to the sound of the choir and letting my gaze rise to the dome overhead, I wondered if the buildings in Heaven might be similar. The space was magnificent, beautiful in design and vibrating with the sounds of Mozart, but it was more than beautiful. It was powerful, and it had a profound effect on me. Something about its age and grandeur, its stone and soaring columns, quieted me, made me feel smaller, and drew my thoughts inward and upward. The space itself moved my spirit and prepared me for the reflection and spiritual engagement I would experience in it.

Similarly, the physical space of your team's environment will inspire the things that happen in it. Like me, you've probably admired the workspaces of premier creative firms like Pixar, IDEO, Facebook, or Google. They're often touted in magazines or presentations and are "tricked out" with progressive architecture, art installations, whimsical décor, games, pets, and recreational areas. They look like all-inclusive resorts for creatives, but they're more purposeful than that. Their unorthodox physical spaces loosen the constraints of convention and lighten the spiritual and emotional load of the people working in them.

That's like giving oxygen to a fire, and it makes these environments creatively flammable. The space itself lifts the heavy corporate atmosphere that might smother creatives' imaginations and encourages them to dream big. If you want your own creatives to be fired up like this, then you need to provide the kinds of physical spaces that breathe life into them.

Culture

If building your own Googleplex sounds a little over the top for your budget, I have good news for you. Physical spaces are only a part of what makes a flammable environment. The creatives in these companies are supported by more than the structural eye candy you see in *Architectural Digest*. They are also inspired by the personal experiences they have with one another each day. These less tangible components of the environment are sometimes referred to as the team's *culture*.

Technically, team culture refers to the system of shared assumptions, values, and beliefs that govern how members behave. But, practically, culture is the hard-to-quantify mixture of mores and behaviors that define the "vibe" of a team. It is described and encouraged through policies, positions, and procedures; but it transcends these things to shape and be shaped by countless informal and individual behaviors every day. I call it "Juju."

Teams with Good Juju seem to move easily and gain momentum quickly. They do extraordinary things because their cultures elevate the vision and capacity of the people in them. Teams with Bad Juju seem to resist movement altogether and need to work hard just to overcome their own inertia. Their cultures have a way of making even the most promising participants smaller, and they seem to live up only to the least inspiring versions of themselves.

Good Juju creates the kind of highly oxygenated atmosphere that makes it easy to kindle a fire in your team, but Bad Juju sucks the air out of a room and the life out of anyone in it. If you walk into an organization with a creative, innovative, and living culture, you know it. You can breathe deeply and feel the Good Juju in the air. It has the telltale scent of opportunity, freedom, and purpose. It's invigorating, like a hit of pure oxygen.

If you want to create the kind of flammable environment that encourages creatives to burn brightly, you need to harness both the physical space and the culture of your team to put wind in your people's sails. Breathe life into them by investing in connections, self-expression, and activity.

Connections

Connections are important because the spark that ignites creativity is often produced by the friction of imaginative people living and working closely with each other. There is a conspicuous creative value in coming together, so you want to make sure the physical spaces and team culture encourage it.

Take stock. Are there common areas and team spaces that foster collaboration and connection? Or does the layout of your work area insulate and isolate your people from each another? It's typical to find workstations and appropriate spaces for individual work, but collaboration needs designated space, too. The Googleplexes of the world have taken this principal to heart and have provided extraordinary opportunities for their employees to connect. My favorite collaborative tool is their "conference bike." One model allows up to twelve people to conduct a meeting while pedaling the same bicycle around Google's park-like campus in Santa Clara, California!

Fortunately, your efforts to support connections environmentally don't require exotic contraptions like this. You may simply need to provide a space for team members to turn away from their work and toward each other during the day.

Figure 1.1

For many years, I worked in an environment that isolated and compartmentalized my team. The physical space encouraged efficiency, not collaboration, and it looked more like a dog kennel than an office suite! It consisted of a long, double-loaded hallway of individual offices off a small reception and lobby area. The only place for team members to connect was a small couch in the lobby area.

During the day, one person or another would drift out to the couch to take a break or regroup from a difficult conversation. Other team members would notice this and join them for a few minutes on the couch.

—

If you want creatives to *connect when it counts,* you need to encourage their connections when it doesn't.

These brief lobby encounters were impromptu opportunities for laughter, commiseration, and amateur therapy. It's where teammates connected and caught up on each other's lives. Then, as spontaneously as the moment arrived, it would end; and people would drift back to their offices again.

These rendezvous were unanticipated and organic, spontaneous reflections of Good Juju that transcended the physical limitations of the space. "Couch Time" became an appreciated and intentional ritual of our team, part of our culture. "I'll meet you for 'couch time' this afternoon..." "We need some 'couch time' on that topic..." "That meeting was awful. I need some 'couch time' to recover..." It was a part of the environment that fostered connection and breathed life into our team. When we eventually remodeled our space, the first thing we added was another couch!

If you want an environment that encourages connection, you also need to consider how your team schedules and spends its time. Do your processes and expectations make it easy for creatives to interact, or do they isolate them from one another? In practice, the most meaningful professional collaborations rest on genuine personal relationships, so you need to make sure personal connections are encouraged and not perceived as unwanted, off-task, or counter-culture.

Put simply: If you want creatives to connect when it counts, you need to encourage their connections when it doesn't. If this commitment isn't consistently reinforced by the environment, you may find that your team lacks the connection it needs to stay fired up.

Recently, I worked with an organization that discovered this the hard way. They had an unwritten policy against impromptu visits to someone else's office or cubicle. They called these encounters "Drive-bys." Team members were encouraged to call ahead or make appointments instead of dropping by to connect with their co-workers unannounced. Presumably, this would ensure that the person they sought would be present when they arrived, and this would prevent wasted trips or missed connections. This intention was laudable. They wanted to foster more reliable connections, but the effect was very different. Instead of enabling more effective connections, the "No Drive-by" policy communicated that it was most important to maximize individual time on task. It recast unplanned interactions as contrary to the team's culture and put an end to spontaneity and visiting altogether.

That's some Bad Juju, and it suffocated some of the fire in their team. If you want to keep your own creatives burning bright, create an environment that fosters connections among them.

Self-Expression

Creatively flammable environments encourage team members to connect with one another, but they also preserve a sense of individualism. Creatives can be smothered by uniformity, and they need some room to express themselves if they are going to continue burning bright. I was reminded of this as I walked into the design department of an organization the other day, and I noticed a professionally printed sign like this one:

Figure 1.2

This seemed like a pretty clear declaration of individuality, but it was made even more emphatic by a crowd of Post-it notes that had been added above and below the word "think." They added to the sentence so that it read "...and don't think, *dress, work, eat, fill out timecards, tell time, leave at five, read, exercise, behave, clean their coffee cups, do meetings, talk quietly, or smell*... like you do." I'm not sure what experiences prompted each of these additions (especially the last one), but one thing is certain. Uniformity was not their goal.

Many popular management philosophies work against self-expression. They're based on the premise that you get the best out of a team when you limit the imperfections and messiness of the "human factor." So they urge leaders to prioritize things like standardization, uniformity, and predictability in the environment. Unfortunately, creativity is fundamentally an act of self-expression, so environments that limit individuality put a lid on imagination, too. And the fire in your team, like the flame on a candle, will go out when the lid is screwed on tight.

The problem is that most of these philosophies were born in the industrial revolution of the early 20th century, and the machine-based, manufacturing-minded model of teamwork they promote is out of sync with the kind of knowledge-based, creative team you are leading today.

In your organization, you're not just looking for increased productivity; you want deeper engagement. That requires you to *unleash* the human factor in your team. Increased control or standardization won't help you as much as embracing individuality and the messiness that comes with it. You need to release the environmental constraints and give creatives room to breathe.

Start with the physical spaces. Nothing says "Uniformity Rules!" or "Think only the thoughts we've thought before!" like the modern "cubical farm." Open office concepts might be a boon to efficiency and space management, but they are hard on individuality. I was asked to speak to a leadership team about innovation recently, and as I was led through their labyrinth of cubicles, I thought to myself, "This is the place where innovation comes to die." I am convinced that if Dante rewrote his "Inferno" today, one ring of Hell would be hosed down in the same non-descript beige color and filled with endless rows of cubicles with identical name-plates and standardized counter-configurations!

It's hard for creatives to express themselves in the physically stultifying effect of those human habitrails, especially if they are reinforced by policies that limit any personalization of the spaces. If you are going to have cubicles or other physical constraints on self-expression, at least encourage creatives to personalize their work areas. Take a lesson from Zappos.

Zappos started as an online shoe company but rapidly rose to dominate that industry and expand into many more. Its success was rooted in self-expression. It transformed a relatively routine and faceless online interaction into a memorable personal experience by encouraging operators to express their individuality. The value of self-expression is woven into the core values of the company:

Deliver WOW Through Service

Embrace and Drive Change

Create Fun and A Little Weirdness

Be Adventurous, Creative, and Open-Minded

Pursue Growth and Learning

Build Open and Honest Relationships With Communication

Build a Positive Team and Family Spirit

Do More With Less

Be Passionate and Determined

Be Humble

Today, the Zappos headquarters contains hundreds of cubicles, but they encourage employees to personalize their workspaces through theme days and contests. In fact, they push it pretty hard. As a result, their employees do some extraordinary things. A walk through their headquarters is like a tour through a theme park where the theme is "Be Yourself." When the environment supports self-expression, it lets the people working in it take a deep breath and be themselves.

Commotion

When your team's culture and its physical space encourage connection and self-expression, the environment isn't always tidy and controlled. It's alive, and when something is alive, it moves around and makes noise. It causes some commotion. If you want to kindle and keep the fire burning in your team, you need to embrace this in your work environment. Of course, too much ruckus can be distracting or inhibit the work that needs to be done. You need to have times and spaces conducive to silent work, but don't let your team's workspace turn into a library reading room, or you'll drive the life out of it and smother the fire in your creatives.

Studies show that, though silence is helpful for certain mental activities, low level noise is better for others, particularly the kind of low volume indistinct noise that stays in the background. This kind of minor distraction actually moves people to greater concentration and increases their creative thought. It's commotion that fires up imagination.

In my own experience, coffeehouses are especially creative environments for this reason. They have the commotion that signals energy and life, but it stays disconnected from me and my laptop. It's there, keeping me awake and energized, but it's not so invasive that it distracts me from my work. This (and the unlimited supply of caffeine) fires me up. If you, too, find the coffeehouse atmosphere inspiring, you can bring it with you. A variety of websites offer you the opportunity to stream the caffeinated commotion wherever you may be. My favorites are soundrown.com and coffitivity.com.

When a team is fired up, they will naturally cause some commotion. It's messy and unpredictable, but it's also engaging and fun. When a fire is burning bright, it's not just the warmth of it that draws people to it and to each other. It's the life. A fire crackles and pops; it dances. And it's this happy commotion that lights up the space, lifts people's spirits, and enlivens their interaction. When was the last time you heard of people sitting around a radiator to sing songs and tell ghost stories?

The point is, some commotion and general "messiness" is a natural outcome of any team that is burning bright, and you want to create an environment that encourages it. How you respond to the "messiness" when it occurs sets a lot of the cultural tone and determines if your environment will fuel or foil creativity.

I was meeting with a project team last week, and our conversation was interrupted by loud laughter in the room beyond. As we continued, we heard some muffled singing followed by more laughter. I had just started to think that I would rather be with the group outside when the leader got up suddenly to address it. "Somebody needs to calm down," he said, as he stepped out the door, and we heard him say pointedly, "You all don't need to be out here. We are trying to meet in here." There was complete silence as he came back into the room.

I couldn't help but think that he had missed an important opportunity to keep the life in his team. He needed to address the distraction for our sake, but the way he did it sucked the oxygen out of the room and reinforced a culture that wasn't conducive to commotion or creativity. Just think of the different kind of culture that would've been revealed or reinforced if he had excused himself by saying, "I'm sorry. Some of our folks are having a lot of fun right now." What different effect would have been achieved if, instead of ordering the noisemakers to leave, he had asked them what was cracking them up? He could've joined them in a laugh and then asked them if they could relocate to avoid distracting the meeting participants.

When something is perpetually present, you grow so accustomed to it that you become unaware of it. For instance, how's the quality of the oxygen you're enjoying right now? Don't know? I'm not surprised. Long ago in your life, you grew accustomed to breathing it, and you're not likely to think about it again unless, of course, it's missing.

It's surprisingly easy to overlook the environment in your leadership for the same reason. You experience the physical spaces and culture of your team every minute, and it's easy to take them for granted. But they often make the difference between a creatively flammable environment and one that's suffocating. When oxygen is missing, you know it immediately because people can't breathe and the fire goes out. So, if you're having trouble kindling or keeping a fire in your team, it may be because your environment isn't encouraging vital things like connection, self-expression, and commotion. Take a closer look and build that highly oxygenated atmosphere that lets them burn.

chapter two

A Dynamic Experience:

Celebrating Ambiguity and Leading In Between

I see my path, but I don't know where it leads. Not knowing where I'm going is what inspires me to travel it.

—Rosalia de Castro

I LOVE TO travel. Over the years, I've visited some interesting and even exotic places, but it's not the destinations that turn me on; it's something about the process of getting to them. I first noticed this in college when the contents of my wallet couldn't take me anywhere close to an exotic destination, but I loved to take trips anyway. My friends and I would pick a random place on the map, load up the car, and start driving. Today, my favorite memories of those trips aren't of where we started or where we finished. They are what we did on the road between the two. I love the In Between.

When you travel, you leave Where You Are and finish Somewhere Else, but for a time you are In Between. The In Between is an adventure; it's unknown and always unfolding in front of you. I suppose this can be said of other times and places in our lives as well, but when we are not In Between, it's less obvious or inspiring. When was the last time a typical Thursday felt like an adventure as you plodded through the usual tasks at your office and stopped for groceries and gas on the way home? Been there, done that, right? Rinse and repeat.

This predictability is the charm and challenge of the familiar situation we call "Home." At Home, everything is known and sure. The people know you, and you know them. You know what to expect, and you know how it works because these are the "givens" in the standard equation of your life. This certainty is reassuring, but it can also become static and uninspiring. It has a way of stabilizing and reaffirming how things are, but then not letting any of them change.

When you go on a trip, you leave Home behind, and you're In Between. It's different there because the givens that hold everything in place get suspended for a while. They'll reassert themselves when you return or when you get to your destination, but while you're In Between, they loosen up or let go altogether. It's like there's more oxygen, more space, and more room to breathe In Between. New options reveal themselves and changes seem easier to make. This is why you come home from trips with new plans for the house, new visions for the future, or new hopes for your kids. In the ambiguity of the In Between, dreams abound, and hope and imagination move more freely.

The In Between & Creatives

The In Between is an especially flammable place for creatives. In the routines of typical organizational life, the press of predictability closes in until there's not enough oxygen left to burn. The ambiguity of the In Between gives creatives room to breathe and fires them up by providing the same sense of motion, surprise, and possibility you feel on a great road trip.

1. Motion

Great road trips aren't about getting someplace, they're about *going* there. The destination often turns out to be just an excuse for the journey. Similarly, creatives are fired up by a sense of going someplace or being in the process even more than by getting there. The product is often less inspiring to them than the process, and they can be surprisingly disinterested in their finished work. I don't mean that they take no pride in what they produce, but while other people marvel at their finished pieces, creatives themselves often treat them like the incidental results of something they love more: creating. That's why creatives like to have multiple projects going at once and why they're likely to dive into a new project quickly when one is finished (or sometimes even when it's not).

This difference between product and process is a subtle but important distinction to keep in mind if you're trying to keep things moving and to keep your creatives' fires burning. The sense of motion they need most isn't about productivity or making more stuff, per se, it's about staying engaged in the creative process. So keep the projects coming. Manage the deadlines, but make sure your team has more than enough to do. Let creatives hop from project to project, and limit their downtime. They need closure and completion along the way, but keeping them immersed in the process of creating will keep them in the In Between and burning bright.

2. Surprise

When I stop for refreshment on a road trip, I like to eat or drink the most local things I can find. I am always surprised by the peculiar array of local sodas and snacks out there, and that's the point, to be surprised. I confess, I've tried some pretty vile concoctions, but I've also discovered some unexpected treats. So I can't help but look for the craziest thing in the Quick Mart when we stop for gas.

Creatives look for new experiences, too. They're not as attracted to the things they've seen or done before, so habit and predictability can bore them and shut them down. You need to keep their experience from becoming too routine, because monotony is a weight that squeezes the oxygen right out of them. Switch things up and surprise them. This doesn't mean that you should be inconsistent or capricious, just interesting. Break up the contents of the day, the shape of the projects, or the look of the room. This creates an experience that is "consistently surprising" and is the paradox that characterizes the In Between and breathes oxygen back into your team.

3. Possibility

Think of the In Between as a windy road to something great. You can't tell what is waiting around each bend until you get there, so you find yourself leaning forward to see it first. On a road trip, it might be a water tower painted like a baseball, a field of sunflowers, or The World's Largest Plastic Cow. Who knows? It could be anything! It's unknown, and it's exciting to discover. Creatives are energized by this same prospect of discovery, so when things get too certain and new possibilities disappear, their enthusiasm does, too. Their experience feels more like driving on the interstate through Kansas on a cloudless day. They can see forever. They might be making good time, but the thrill is gone quickly, and they find themselves glazing over and tuning out.

If you want to keep your team leaning forward and looking ahead, you need to preserve the sense of possibility they feel. You fire them up when you keep options open and resist the urge to settle things too quickly. Set goals, but leave room for creatives to determine their own routes or the detours that turn them on. Celebrate the discoveries that happen along the way and be willing to change course when promising new possibilities arise.

It's easier to kindle and keep a fire in creatives when their experience is characterized by a sense of motion, surprise, and possibility because this enriches the In Between. They want you to take them on an epic trip, and that's more about the journey than the destination. So sometimes you just need to loosen your grip on the wheel, look out the window, and say, "Hey, let's take a detour to see the World's Largest Plastic Cow!"

Leading in the In Between

Unfortunately, loosening your grip and investing in the journey is difficult. The ambiguity of the In Between might be an invigorating space for creatives, but it can feel threatening and uncomfortably out of control for the person leading them. The difference may be due to personality—leaders and creatives can be wired differently—but more likely it is a function of the difference in their roles and perspectives. Leaders tend to focus on the goal, but teams tend to focus on the process.

When I am a passenger on a road trip, I'm just "along for the ride" and looking for adventures along the way. I'm the one who wants to take the road that doesn't show up on the GPS or the detour to see that plastic cow. However, when I'm behind the wheel and driving the car, I'm the guy who makes sure we stay on track. I use the GPS to determine the shortest route,

I time the bathroom breaks, and I avoid detours and tourist traps like the plague. Similarly, creatives are typically immersed in the journey, while their leaders are nervously eyeing the distance to the destination.

Leaders feel the responsibility of getting everyone where they are supposed to go, and they like to minimize the possibility of slowing down or getting sidetracked along the way. This makes it difficult for them to tolerate the ambiguity and unpredictability that characterizes the In Between. Instead, they work hard to maximize their control and increase certainty. When they drive the ambiguity out, it's like sucking the oxygen out of the room, and they inadvertently damage the opportunity and possibility creatives need to stay fired up.

If you've felt this tension as a leader yourself, take courage. Being In Between is not the same as being lost. Your team's experience can be unpredictable and still be headed in the right direction. To support the ambiguity that fuels creativity, you don't need to create chaos or lose your bearings altogether. You just need to relax your grip a little. Here are two counter-intuitive strategies to help you embrace ambiguity in your leadership and preserve the parts of the In Between that breathe life into your team.

1. Hold on loosely to your expectations

Many of the leaders I coach have "long distance radar." I mean that they are often able to see things coming from far away. They have a knack for anticipating future events and then positioning themselves to meet challenges or to make the most of opportunities before they arise. Curiously, this ability is a hallmark of both the best and worst leaders I know. It's not the ability to predict the future that differentiates the two; it is how tightly they hold on to their predictions as they advance.

The most successful leaders I know hold on to their predictions loosely. They maintain a fragile confidence that what they *believe* will happen will *actually occur*. This doesn't mean that they are ambivalent or confused. In fact, they trust their foresight enough to base their actions and decisions on it in the present. (This is why they seem to be already poised for new challenges and opportunities when they arise.) However, despite their confidence in their predictions, these leaders are also vigilant for things to change along the way. They know that life is a fluid proposition and that even their best guesses of where it's headed are subject to change after the next action or inaction. So they keep their radar running even as they are putting their plans in motion. They acknowledge and embrace ambiguity by simultaneously stepping toward the future they expect and watching for it to change during the In Between.

The less successful leaders I know often have the same ability to anticipate the future, but they put too much confidence in their predictions and end up limiting their opportunity as a result. They ignore the ambiguity of the In Between and lock themselves into an artificially static picture of a future that may or may not bear out. This confidence makes a person feel more in control, but it limits their strategic opportunities instead of broadening them. For example, if you anticipate how someone might respond to a proposal before you make it, your foresight will enable you to design the pitch more effectively. However, if you let your mental posture slip from appreciating the *likelihood* of a particular response to anticipating it as a "given," you're no longer considering possibilities; you're making assumptions.

Acting on assumptions can get you and your team in trouble. This approach is like using your radar to anticipate what is likely to happen, but then switching it off and charging blindly down that path. In keeping with the oxygen metaphor, it's like holding your breath and forging ahead when you need to keep breathing along the way. This kind of misplaced certainty leads you to one of two disappointing conclusions: you either miss what you most hope for, or you get what you least desire.

In some cases, you miss what you most hope for because you are holding on to your expectations too tightly and you don't notice when new factors or other forces alter the future you envisioned. The equation you solved changes and leaves your calculations misplaced. If this happens, your team will complete their preparations and positioning just as you had planned, only to find that the opportunity they anticipated never materialized, or that it already passed them by.

In other cases, you get what you least desire because a leader's perspective on the future has a way of turning possibilities into reality for better or for worse. If you don't embrace the ambiguity of the In Between, it's easy to cross the line between *positioning* for possible future events and actually *causing* them. Of course, it's wise to gear up for the difficulties or problems you see on the horizon and position your team to meet or avoid them, but it is important to realize that the problems you've *anticipated* haven't actually occurred yet. When you're In Between, the future isn't certain.

If you act too assertively in the present to position yourself for the bad things you anticipate, you often raise the load and anxiety of your team unnecessarily. Or worse, you make a self-fulfilling prophesy that creates the very future you wanted to avoid. This is deadly for you and your team because it creates a vicious cycle in which you keep getting what you least desire because you are manufacturing it yourself!

To protect your team from missing what it most hopes for and getting what it least desires, you need to embrace the ambiguity that comes with being In Between and resist rushing to certainty too soon. Keep your eye on the future so that you'll have a picture of what's possible, but keep the air—the oxygen—in the system and let things breathe. Hold on loosely to your expectations, and remind yourself that your picture of the future is possible, maybe even probable, but not certain. You'll be able to refine that picture and your preparations more effectively if you stay open to alternatives as you advance.

2. Slow Down Your Impulse to Control

If holding on too tightly to your expectations drives the oxygen, or opportunity, out of the system cognitively, then acting too quickly to control things does the same thing physically, with the same negative consequences. The fire in your team will go out.

The In Between is an inherently ambiguous place. That means that situations are frequently not what they seem, and first impressions are misleading. To lead well in such an uncertain and dynamic environment, you need to let things breathe a little before exerting your control. Slow down and take stock. The situation might change, or you might come to a new understanding of it if you resist the urge to control it right away. To twist a familiar adage into a more applicable shape, *don't just do something, sit there.*

Unfortunately, "sitting there" even for a short time, goes against the instincts of most leaders. It's their nature to act when they see problems, needs, or loose ends, and it's this inclination that often distinguishes them from everyone else. If you're in a leadership role, it's probably this bias for action that won you the opportunity to lead in the first place. Earlier in your career, when problems arose and others stepped back, you stepped up; and that assertiveness distinguished you as worthy of greater responsibility and authority.

Your inclination to act is important. Your team is looking for courage and initiative at the top, and they want you to assert control over the things that threaten their success. However, some of the same dispositions that make you comfortable stepping up and taking control may also make it difficult for you to step back or tolerate the unknown and unsettled things that characterize the In Between and keep the fire burning in your team. I understand that it feels lazy or irresponsible to let loose ends lie and that you want to act fast to tie them up, but resist that urge. Fast, decisive action often removes the oxygen creatives need to burn and makes the situation worse. Sometimes the choice *not* to act isn't lazy; its leadership.

It often feels good and "leaderly" to take charge, but fast action usually addresses only the symptoms of deeper, more threatening issues. Sometimes, a slower response, or even no response at all, is a better move, because it permits the source of problems to emerge from the symptoms and it encourages others to step in or step up. An overly assertive response can also set in motion a cycle that makes a problem worse instead of better. When this happens, leaders don't usually recognize their own roles in escalating the problems they're trying to address. They continue to believe they are responding to threats when they are actually initiating them, and as the problem worsens, they double down on the choices they've already made. Of course, this makes the situation worse and prompts even more aggressive action on their part. Ironically, this kind of impulsive action by leaders often improves the *immediate* situation even as it contributes to the longer-term problem. Leaders that are moving too fast to consider the full implications of their actions see only the short term gain, and they become even more convinced that assertive action is always best.

In general, kindling and keeping the fire in your team requires you to embrace the messy and unresolved nature of the In Between. The loose ends, multiple meanings, and uncertainty that often make you feel uncomfortable as a leader are often the very things that give your team the sense of motion, surprise, and possibility that lets the fire in creatives breathe. This is the tension you manage whenever you lead creatives. Start fanning the flames now by relaxing your grip on your expectations and resisting your impulse to control.

chapter three

Room to Breathe:

Managing Margin for Productivity, Innovation, and Resilience

A great secret of success is to go through life as a man who never gets used up.

—Albert Schweitzer

LATELY, I'VE BEEN struggling to fit my life into my life. There's just too much of it and too little of me. You probably know the feeling, too. Your To-Do list is bursting at the seams, and for each entry you've managed to check off, you've added three more. You've put your own world on hold and stolen time from every other role and relationship you have. Some time ago, you passed the point of being able to improve your situation by simply managing better and working harder. You've exhausted the hours in your day and your "go to" strategies for taming your To-Do list. No matter what lengths you've gone to or which compromises you've made, you can't seem to handle everything; and there seems to be no end in sight. It's like drinking from a fire hose, and you stopped being thirsty a long time ago.

I call this chaotic and overwhelming experience the Season of the Fire Hose. It sounds a little extreme when it's written on a page like this, but I bet it sounds familiar to you. I bet you even felt your pulse quicken or your shoulders tighten as you read it. The Season of the Fire Hose is a natural consequence of elevated aspirations and authority, so the only way to be free from it (short of winning the lottery and becoming a hermit) is to try to be, and to do, very little. As appealing as that might sound, for most leaders it's about as feasible as the hermit gig. For leaders of creatives, the Season of the Fire Hose is especially threatening because kindling and keeping your team's fire burning is hard to do when the fire hose is trying to put it out.

Making Margin

In the Season of the Fire Hose, life is too full and people have trouble keeping up and coping because they don't have room to breathe. The fire in them dwindles, and they find themselves gasping for oxygen in the wash of everything they have to do. They need something called "margin."

Margin is the space between a person's total capacity and the amount of it that is being used at the time. It's the unused portion of the whole that lets things breathe. On a printed page, the empty space at the edge, between paragraphs, and around pictures helps the reader organize, prioritize, and pace the content it contains. Without it, you'd be overwhelmed and have trouble making sense of it all. In your life, the empty or unprogrammed moments in your day or week do the same thing. They give you the breathing room you need to reflect, recharge, or make sense of everything else your busy life contains. Without them, you'll find yourself moving grimly from one thing to the next with no real sense of the whole. This leftover space in your schedule, your thoughts, or your emotional capacity is your margin. It's like the oxygen that lets you breathe and find the space for reflection and rejuvenation in the midst of everything else. This kind of space is critical to your team's innovation, productivity, and resilience.

Margin & Innovation

When creatives' time and attention are oversubscribed, they lack margin, and their perspective changes in a way that specifically sabotages innovation. They shift from imagining the best possibilities and the greatest outcomes to merely trying to make it through their day. When the air is gone in their schedules, the pressure of immediate things supplants any thoughts about future ones, and they become less interested in what they are trying to accomplish, even as they become preoccupied with what they are required to do. When margin is missing, a Tyranny of the To-Do list takes over, which draws creatives into the minutia of the moment. It kills your calls for innovation not by directly confronting or refuting them, but by simply overwhelming and eclipsing them.

Innovation depends upon reflection and imagination, but both of these disappear when individual capacity gets pressed too far and people focus more on survival than exploration. They can't risk wild goose chases or mental forays that don't pan out. Instead of imagining new futures or exploring unexpected routes to them, marginless people try to map the shortest paths between two points. This shuts down innovation and originality, because dreaming isn't an efficient process and well-worn paths only lead to equally worn destinations.

When creatives lack margin, there isn't enough oxygen to support the spark of imagination, let alone a good burn. They aren't able to make the unusual connections that constitute creative thought, and their busyness produces only derivative or uninspired results. They don't need more meetings and management; they need more margin. Stop the pep talks and inspiring speeches, and start making space in their schedules if you want to keep them burning bright.

Margin & Productivity

Freeing up your creatives' time and taking things off their To-Do lists may sound counterproductive to you. After all, in the Season of the Fire Hose, you need full engagement, and this feels like you're taking your foot off the gas and failing to get everything out of everyone. It's hard not to push everyone to their limit when resources are tight and the productivity of your team is the measure of your own performance. But if you want creatives to burn their brightest, they need margin, and margin exists only when they function below their absolute maximum capacity.

Try recalibrating your concept of what it means to be "fully engaged" to include margin. Let me give you a picture to illustrate this idea. Each time I order coffee at my local coffeehouse, the barista asks me if I want "room." By this, she is asking me if I'd like her to leave space in the cup for me to add cream. I always answer, "No," not because I don't plan on adding cream, but because I'm greedy and I'm trying to get as much in my cup as possible. She hands me a cup that is filled to about three-quarters of an inch from the top with coffee. Technically, this is not "full," so I proceed to top it off with half-and-half. I fill it right up to the brim. To be honest, I'm especially proud if I manage to get it even slightly above the brim of the cup. (Don't pretend that you've never tried this...) "Now that's full!" I think, and as I congratulate myself and try to take a sip, I spill it on the counter, on my clothes, or on the poor guy next to me.

It's really not a complicated problem, but it happens all the time. I simply cannot recalibrate my notion of what "full" really means. My caffeine-craving brain can't seem to grasp the reality that my cup's *functional* capacity is some amount less than its finite capacity. If I want to avoid a big mess, then I need to ask for "room" and resist the urge to max it out. Last week, I literally drew a line on the outside of my cup to remind myself that "full" includes margin!

Like my coffee cup, your creatives' functional capacity is somewhat less than their finite capacity, and if you fill them to the brim, you may have a mess on your hands. Rethink what it means for someone to be productive or fully engaged, and then factor in some "room." Just because they can take on another project doesn't mean they should. Just because they have some time available doesn't mean you should fill it. They are fully engaged before they are working at full capacity. Maybe you need to figuratively draw a different line for yourself so that you know when consuming more of their capacity will produce diminished returns.

This discipline is especially tricky with your top performers, because it is always tempting to give them more. When they're busy, they're still your best bets, and as the saying goes, the reward for good work is more work. But be careful; when margin disappears, there are no more reserves to allocate. The only way they can take on more is to borrow from the time they've already committed. This means that if you keep adding work to your top performers, you will pass the point of diminished returns and start trading quality for quantity. Cannibalizing their own commitments frustrates creatives who want to do their best and quickly turns your top performers into average **ones**.

Margin & Resilience

In addition to supporting innovation and productivity, margin makes your team more resilient and able to endure. Think of it this way: If margin provides breathing room, facing challenges without it is like trying to run a marathon while holding your breath. You need oxygen to go the distance and to handle the hills along the way. Similarly, margin enables your team to endure and to bounce back more quickly and completely from the difficulties, setbacks, and disappointments that naturally accompany the creative process. Without it, their resilience decreases and they become brittle. Surprisingly, small things can break or derail them, and they become wary of investing any more.

To maximize the resilience of your team, resist the urge to rev your creatives to the max. Allowing them to step back from the blast of the fire hose now and then lets them get a breath, increases their endurance, and gives them the ability to step forward again when you need it most. There will be times when you will call on them to make extraordinary commitments of their time and energy in the interest of a goal, but this should be relatively rare. If this kind of sacrificial contribution is expected on a regular basis, team members will soon be ill-equipped to do anything more than survive. Instead, encourage them to maintain their margin so they will have something extra to offer when it's needed.

In general, creatives' efforts to maintain their margin are an important investment in both stamina and outcomes. A team that I work with reminds its members of this in an interesting way. They believe that when people reach the limits of themselves, they lose self-awareness and make bad decisions, so they encourage their team members to HALT before making important choices or commitments.

This acronym reminds creatives that they are probably not at their best if they are Hungry, Angry, Lonely, or Tired, and it gives them permission to care for these things before attending to the task. It encourages them to delay action or step back from demands if they need to increase their capacity to do them well. They might need to have a candy bar, calm down, connect with confidantes, or simply rest and recharge before they continue; and the HALT routine makes sure they do it. It is this organization's way of systematically elevating the importance of margin and preventing its people from drowning in front of the fire hose.

You might want to use the HALT idea to remind your creatives that they make the best choices and contributions when they aren't at the limits of themselves, and also that you support them in doing what it takes to bring their very best.

If you're looking for more innovation, productivity, or resilience in your team, you may need to make more margin. Adding a little breathing room is often like adding oxygen to a fire, and it fans the flames of creativity. Unfortunately, like oxygen, margin is hard to appreciate until it's gone. As a result, we don't take good care of it. We squander it when we have it, and we continue to make commitments or spread ourselves thinner after we've passed the point of optimal performance and are gasping for air. In that spot, it is especially hard to make margin because it feels like we're being irresponsible or letting others down. We are reluctant to leave some task undone, some base uncovered, and we end up trapped by our own sense of obligation.

If you or your team is experiencing the Season of the Fire Hose now, you can't afford to wait until making margin is comfortable or consequence-free. That moment never seems to come, and you will end up desperate and drowning while you wait. Brace yourself, take stock of your capacity and start backing away from the edge now. The courage and discipline you model for your team will help the creatives lean against the flow in their own lives. When it comes to building margin and adding oxygen to your life, every little bit counts, and you will see improved productivity, innovation, and resilience as the fire rises in your team.

chapter four

Conditions for Volition:

Maintaining Your Power to Choose When Margin Is Missing

Everything can be taken from a man but one thing: the last of human freedoms—to choose one's attitude in any given set of circumstances, to choose one's own way.

— Viktor E. Frankl

IF YOU'RE ONE of the leaders for whom the Season of the Fire Hose is a daily or abiding condition, you're in a bad spot. There's no sugarcoating it. An unrelenting diet of that kind of stress, where you find yourself marginless and operating beyond the bounds of your capacity, is a recipe for failure—if not your team's, then your own. Try as you might, you can't keep their fire burning if yours is going out. If you can't change the equation and stop the madness, you will have only two choices: barricade yourself for a heroic last stand or get out. Systems that have become inherently consuming are predatory, and they aren't going to change on their own. They are self-amplifying and, barring some cataclysmic event (a leadership change, a market reversal, or a seismic shift in the givens), they will devour any and all resources in their path, including you.

Fortunately, most of us aren't in such a dire spot; we just feel like it. Or more precisely, we *are* in that spot, but only for a while. I want to offer a few strategies to help you survive and to help you serve your team well in the midst of it. Think of these strategies as your own personal oxygen tank. They will keep your fire burning when the wash of all those other things threatens to put it out.

The Season of the Fire Hose is especially hard on leaders because it brings more than just hard work. It brings the kind of unrelenting barrage that makes you feel like you've lost control and your life is running you. That means you lose your sense of volition, the confidence that you can exercise your own will and make choices. Simply put, the fire hose makes you feel like a victim, and people aren't wired to function very well for very long as victims.

It's not necessarily the sheer quantity of the work that makes you feel this way. It is the disproportionate amount of your life that is consumed by it. It's not the number of demands you face, but how the rest of your life feels connected or subordinated to them that defines your sense of purpose and control. You're capable of making extravagant commitments of emotion and energy and of devoting impressive quantities of time and attention, as long as the object of those investments seems part of a bigger personal picture. But when the immediate demands start eclipsing the bigger picture or making you doubt if there even is a bigger picture, your efficacy and endurance run out quickly.

The important internal stuff that helps you rise to demands and bounce back from challenges in normal seasons disappears, and you run out of gas. When that happens, your heroic efforts to make margin for others by taking on more work yourself boomerang and become counterproductive, because they deplete the courage and capacity you need to make more hard choices down the road. If you want to keep the fire burning in your creatives during the Season of the Fire Hose, you need to nurture your own sense of control. Here are some tips for fanning the flames of your own volition when the Fire Hose threatens to put them out.

Make Additions for Volition

When you are feeling overwhelmed, it's tempting to think that the solution lies in limiting the demands that come your way, but this isn't very realistic in the Season of the Fire Hose. If you could turn down the flow of the hose, you would have already. Fortunately, when you can't turn down the flow of the Fire Hose, you can improve your experience by changing the proportion of your life that it consumes. Maintaining your volition requires you to adjust the balance of the things in your life rather than the sheer volume. This means that you can often add to your life beyond your work to make sure there continues to be a "bigger picture."

I realize that adding something to your already over-filled life may sound crazy, like telling folks in the path of a flood that the secret to survival isn't diminishing the water as much as it is adding to the dry land, but that's exactly what I'm saying. When it feels like your job is running your life, you don't need more strategies to manage the work; you need to change your perspective. In fact, the strategies you rely on to improve efficiency and fit more into your day during normal seasons can be dangerous traps in the Season of the Fire Hose, because they suck you deeper into the insatiable demands that are already overwhelming you. You can only manage better and work smarter for so long. After that, only a change in your perspective can give you a renewed sense of capacity and control.

Here are some counterintuitive tips that may add more to your day but will create a greater sense of capacity and control in the end. They're not designed to give you less to do or to make you more efficient. They're designed to keep you from feeling like a victim and to prepare you to make choices for yourself and your team.

Add to the part of your life that has nothing to do with work. Take the minutes you feel like you don't have and spend them on something you care about or something that serves your aspirations, interests, or loves. It doesn't need to take long or be dramatic to make a difference. It just needs to be about you and yours, instead of about "them" and "theirs." Even small decisions in this direction make a difference because it puts the Fire Hose in its place. When you prioritize your personal interests, it reminds you that you actually have some, and it restores your confidence that you can make choices about where you spend the best of yourself.

RECONNECT WITH THE PEOPLE YOU LOVE. Have a meal with a "significant other" you remember caring about before the Season of the Fire Hose started. It may be hurried or squeezed between other commitments, but it's worlds different than a cereal bar at your desk or skipping the meal altogether. It's not really about nutrition anyway; it's about recalibration. It's about reconnecting with relationships that sustain you and reminding yourself that there is more to your life than drinking from the hose.

DO SOME CHORES AROUND THE HOUSE. When margin gets thin, these are the first things you're likely to put on hold because they don't affect anyone else, but eventually, such selflessness feels like less and less of a choice. Prioritizing some of those back-burner items can remind you that you're still in charge. Believe it or not, it can feel good to do the laundry or the dishes because it's *your* laundry and *your* dishes, and you're letting the Hose know where it stands. More importantly, you're letting yourself know that you won't sacrifice everything in your life to its flood.

DO SOME OF YOUR HOME CHORES OR PROJECTS BEFORE YOU GO TO WORK. It needn't be anything big, but it needs to be something about *your* home, *your* life. If you wake up in the morning with the primary goal of getting to work, it's not long before it feels like work is your native environment and home is just the place you go to sleep for a little while in between. That's a dangerous polarity. Recalibrate to remind yourself that your home and your life is your native environment and that work is simply a place you go for a while (even if it's a long while) each day. You will feel less victimized by the raw amount of time you spend at work when you remember that work is only a portion of the greater and grander scheme of your whole life.

ADD SOMETHING THAT MATTERS. Sometimes, the most debilitating aspect of the Season of the Fire Hose is not that it fills too much of our time, but that it satisfies too little of our desire for meaning. It's easy to be consumed by urgent demands that don't seem to matter, and we need to matter. We can do amazing things and be remarkably resilient when we are convinced that we are serving something significant, but we quickly feel small and empty when we believe our endeavors are insignificant. Add a meaningful task to your week that serves someone, advances a cause, or makes a difference in the world.

Build a Levee

Sometimes, improving the balance in your life and restoring your sense of volition isn't about adding personal things; it's about protecting the ones that are already there. By this I mean that if you want to keep the fire burning, it's important to safeguard the priorities, commitments, and relationships you burn for. The Season of the Fire Hose is ravenous and has a way of consuming any role or relationship you leave unattended. If you don't take steps to protect or preserve the important things, you'll find them in shambles when the Season eventually passes.

Occasionally, my wife reminds me of this by telling me she's getting only "leftovers." She means that the best of me is getting used up in the flood, and I'm only offering her what hasn't gotten washed away already. I hate those conversations because she's almost always right. She puts up with recurrent Seasons of the Fire Hose admirably and supports me despite my depletion and preoccupation during them. I want to give her the best of me in return, but there's not a lot of me left. She often ends up suffering through the Season of the Fire Hose once removed, as my priorities get commandeered and she's eventually not among them.

She's not content with that, and neither am I. I've learned that, to prevent this, I need more than good intentions; I need some boundaries. I need some levees in my life to keep the Fire Hose's effects from extinguishing my fire and pouring into every last corner and relationship. Levees may not actually shorten or temper the Season of the Fire Hose itself, but they will provide a little shelter for the things I hope to have and to hold when it ebbs.

Levees can take many forms, but I've found some of the most important ones control communication. They keep the information and interruption of work from supplanting personal interactions with the important people in your life. They are small but important commitments not to discuss certain topics in certain contexts (no "shoptalk" in bed), to leave the cellphone in the car for the duration of your son's soccer game, to text or make a five-minute "how's-your-day" call to your wife midday, to let voicemail do its job during dinner, to stay late but leave the work at the office, or to come home for dinner even if you will need to leave again later.

Embarrassingly, I've learned that I even need to protect the opportunity to communicate with myself. If I am not careful, the rush of my life distances me from my own thoughts, and I lose touch with me! When I don't know my own priorities, I am easily pushed around by others' and fail to lead my team well. For this reason, I prioritize the time I spend over a cup of coffee before work each morning. It is not necessarily long or leisurely, but it is sacred because it takes place before I step into the wash of the Fire Hose and because it gives me a chance to catch up with myself. My secretary preserves it in my schedule, my wife resists filling it with chores, and I personally keep the demands of the day at bay until it's over. It's the time for me to tune in to me. I even get up earlier when I have early appointments to ensure a few minutes of "coffee time" first.

There's nothing magical about coffee—well, I suppose caffeine comes close to being magical some mornings—but the real magic lies in the ability of this short time to conjure in me the sense that I am more than my schedule, that I choose this life and this season because it is important to me. For a few minutes, I build a levy and impose my own life and the things I say I value on the rush of other demands that frequently sweeps them into the neglected nooks and crannies of my schedule. I figuratively close the door to the rest of my day and barricade it against the barrage that is building up outside. After years of this habit, it's a pretty watertight door, and I enjoy imagining the Hose blasting the outside of it, splashing everywhere to no avail. After a few minutes and a last swallow, I take a deep breath, open the door, and start pushing into the flow again.

You may need a dry space like this in your schedule, too, a little time to collect yourself and remind yourself of what you value in the midst of the busyness. The opportunity for personal reflection will help you get and keep your bearings, but, more importantly, the discipline of protecting these brief moments will renew your sense of volition.

One of the most important levees I maintain is an imaginary boundary I cross on my drive home from the office. Like many of you, I continue to drink from the Fire Hose via cellphone even if I manage to escape the office at a reasonable hour. It's my way of eeking out just a little more time on task as I commute. But when I pass the Concord Road interstate exit ten minutes from my home, the eeking stops. It's a sort of line of demarcation, a skirmish line signaling the boundary of my personal life. When I pass it, an imaginary alarm is raised, and I recall that I need to protect the things on the other side, so I hang up. I turn away from the Fire Hose not because it has stopped running, but because I need the remainder of my drive to shake off the water and remember what it's like to be a husband and father and friend with interests and concerns other than swallowing as fast as I can.

I take this boundary line seriously. I cling desperately to this levee like a man in the path of a flood, because it is one of the few things that protects me and mine from the full brunt of the Season of the Fire Hose. More than one of my team has heard me say, "Coming up on Concord... Gotta go... *click.*" I've even pulled over to the side of the road before the exit in order to finish an important conversation, because once the exit's behind me, the Fire Hose is as well. I know it's held only temporarily at bay, and I can still hear its roar, but it's in the distance and not as distracting. I am reminded that I can choose my own focus for a time.

———

The margin you build in *your own life* becomes the personal reserve you draw from to support and encourage your team and keep them burning bright.

All of this effort to prioritize and protect your own interests and commitments during the Season of the Fire Hose may come across as self-serving, but it's not. In fact, it's one of the best investments you can make in the interest of the people who are counting on you to lead them well. Your team needs a leader who is willing and able to make hard choices, not a victim pushed around by the pressure of the Fire Hose. Any effort to boost your own volition gives you more of it to exercise on their behalf. So managing the margin—the oxygen—in your own life prepares you to breathe life into your team when they need it most.

You get a reminder of this principle each time you fly. The attendant tells you that if you are traveling with small children or someone who needs assistance, you should place the oxygen mask on yourself before assisting them. The first time I heard this, I remember thinking, "Well, that's pretty selfish," but of course it isn't. If you try to be a hero and fail to take care of yourself first, you'll pass out and be of no use to anyone. Similarly, your commitment to maintain your own sense of volition during the Season of the Fire Hose prepares you to help others maintain theirs. The margin you build in your own life becomes the personal reserve you draw from to support and encourage your team and keep them burning bright.

chapter five

An Open Horizon:

Posing Three Questions to Keep Reality at Bay

Reality is wrong. Dreams are for real.

                                                    —Tupac Shakur

TAKE A LOOK at how children draw landscapes, and
you'll see something interesting. When a five- or six-
year-old draws a picture of their house or some other
outdoor scene, they draw grass on the bottom third of
the paper and sky and a smiling sun on the top third
of the paper, but they leave a gap of empty paper in between. There might be a house, a school, some people
hanging out on the grass, or some birds or a plane in
the sky, but there is a big empty space separating them.
What is that space? Check out the masterpieces of little artists on the refrigerator or kindergarten bulletin
boards, and you won't be able to find the horizon. The
sky and the ground simply don't meet. As the artists get
older, the sky and ground in their pictures creep toward
each other until one day they touch, and their pictures
look more or less like reality from then on.

   This makes me a little sad, because I am convinced
imagination lives in that undefined space between the

sky and the ground. Kids have an abundance of it when they are young. Anything can happen, pretending is easy, and the world is filled with unexpected delights and new opportunities. As they mature, they get real and see the world as it is. They learn that there are rules that apply and limit the possibilities. Pretending gets a little harder, and that precious undefined space in their drawings disappears.

I suppose it's not all bad. When you need to live in a world that can be altogether too real, it's important to learn the way things really are, what to expect, and how to conduct yourself. But I think it's important to be able to suspend the rules and live a little less realistically, as well. Creatives think so, too, and they maintain their imaginations in part by refusing to see things simply as they are. They need your help to push back reality and preserve the opportunity to create. Metaphorically, they need you to keep some air between the sky and ground and to give them the oxygen they need to burn.

Pressure for Productivity

Unfortunately, it can be hard to preserve the opportunity to create in the press of organizational activity and expectations. Most organizations are more concerned about being productive than about being creative, and this pressure for productivity is tough on creatives because it pushes them to find the shortest path between two points. In this endeavor, unknown and undiscovered things become dangerous diversions or unproductive distractions, and creatives find themselves confined to the most prescribed or well-worn routes. The pressure to get more done faster shuts down their imagination and discourages them from asking questions about the paths they are taking, let alone the destinations to which they lead.

Too much pressure on productivity drives the oxygen right out of the room and creatives wither, because they need the opportunity to ask questions and take unexpected turns. The status quo anchors them in time and place, and they need you to release this mooring so their imaginations can soar beyond the givens. Those givens are dangerous or even deadly to imagination because they define what *is*, and the flames of creativity are fanned by entertaining and exploring what *might be*. If you want your team to burn brightly, then you need to encourage it to transcend the givens. Three questions can help you keep reality at bay and give their imaginations room to breathe: "What *could* it be?" "What *would* it be?" and "What *should* it be?"

What could it be?

This question unleashes the power of prediction in your team. It frees imagination from the reality of the present and lets it run off into the future. It shakes off the grip of the status quo and encourages creatives to entertain what *might* be without factoring in the weights and constraints of what already *is*.

Asking, "What could it be?" is like a breath of fresh air. It encourages creatives to dream without boundaries, and they need your encouragement because there are always boundaries—money is tight, time is short, the room isn't the right size, the lighting is bad, the weather doesn't cooperate, or the supplies are hard to find. You know these boundaries because you've bumped into them countless times yourself. As the leader, it's your job to help your team's imagination transcend them. There are scores of other well-meaning people waiting to give creatives notes and bring them back to reality. Your team looks to you for the champion who will keep reality and the realists at bay long enough for them to dream. Preserving that opportunity is vital if you want creativity to flourish, because when reality drives our dreaming, it usually doesn't travel far from home. We end up only tweaking things that already exist or making minor variations on common themes instead of coming up with something genuinely new.

When you ask, "What could it be?" you give your team permission to leave reality behind, at least temporarily. You suspend the givens that invisibly tether them to known paths and expected things, and you invite them to think about what they would create if there weren't such limitations. This is especially hard to do when the clock is ticking loudly and supervisors or clients are clamoring for results. It's easy to think that factoring the limitations into the dreaming at the start will keep you from wasting time on infeasible ideas. It might, but when it comes to fanning the flames of creativity, feasibility is overrated.

There will be time to consider the limitations carefully, but that time is after the dreaming, not during it, because it's being unencumbered by reality that lets imagination soar. After it has soared to an extraordinary new place, you can always introduce feasibility concerns. You can consider how close you can get to the target with your current resources, opportunities, etc. You may even discover that you can take only a few steps in that direction, but at least you have a truly inspiring vision to pursue. Creatives are happier grappling with the challenges of distant but exceptional dreams than they are walking predictable paths to uninspired ones. You will keep them fired up when you keep asking them, "What could it be?"

What would it be?

This question focuses your team on the promise of potential and is all about connecting with a future state. One of the reasons reality is so limiting is because it is frozen in time. *What it is* doesn't move or change or grow; it just is. It's like a snapshot, figures frozen in time with no past and no future, no potential. When you ask, "What would it be?" you are freeing yourself and your team from this stasis and imagining what would happen if the idea or project continued to develop unconstrained. It's as if you reveal that the snapshot you were considering is only one frame of a longer film, and you ask creatives to imagine what it will look like by the end of the reel.

Creativity is a generative process focused on birthing new ideas or breathing new life into old ones. This means that, though it may be rooted in the things that are present in the status quo, it is always pushing them forward and pressing for future states. When you ask, "What would it be?" you direct your team's attention beyond the current state to future possibilities. This grants the idea or project a life of its own and asks creatives to imagine how it will grow or where it will go as it matures. It's like asking them to look at an acorn and imagine an oak tree. For that matter, it's like asking them to imagine a tire swing, a treehouse, and three generations of squirrels that your daughter names after Disney characters. You get the idea.

When you ask, "What would it be?" you challenge creatives to envision more, not simply to produce more, and that's good because overemphasizing productivity can harm their ability to see the future. Paradoxically, there is something about the pressure to make progress that draws people's attention closer to where they are at the moment. You can see this in practice if you've ever gone hiking with a group. If it's a leisurely outing with no real pressure to get someplace, participants look around at each other, scan the path ahead, and enjoy the scenery. But if there are time constraints or other pressures, their gaze drops quickly, and their field of vision narrows until they're looking only at their own boots or the path in front of their feet. You need your team to have a different posture. You want them eying the horizon.

In my experience, new endeavors are usually birthed with big visions, but these visions dwindle quickly as the future becomes constrained by the present and the reality of what *is* begins to temper and diminish the image of what *would* be. That's when the team's posture slips, its gaze drops, and it loses its vision for the projects and programs it pursues. So be wary of the predatory present. Breathe oxygen into their imagination and refresh their visions of the future by asking them, "What would it be?"

What should it be?

This final question fires up your team by emphasizing the priority of purpose. If the first two questions released the artificial constraints on creatives' minds, this one frees the fetters on their hearts because it is all about connecting with conviction.

The status quo is an imperfect package sold to us "as is" by our leaders and our circumstances. We know there are no refunds or returns, so we try hard to make the best of it. This might be a useful coping mechanism for some people, but it initiates a slow death for creatives because it urges them to resign themselves to the limits of reality and to settle for so much less than what *should* be.

What *should be* is important to creatives because the process of creation isn't simply one of organizing and actualizing miscellaneous preferences—choosing one word or phrase over another, picking a particular shade of green, widening or tightening the shot—it's much deeper and existential than that. To non-creatives, choices like these seem arbitrary or like mere matters of execution. To creatives, they feel more personal, more meaningful. At their best, creatives aren't trying to simply move projects forward; they're trying to move them in the directions they *ought* to go. The choices they make in that regard aren't incidental or casual; they're purposeful. They are expressions of conviction more than demonstrations of expertise.

If you want to fire up your creatives, you need to remember that there is a lot riding on their choices. Encourage them to imagine the best-case scenario for every one. Urge them to connect to their convictions and to imagine how things should be in a perfect world. Of course, the world is far from perfect, and they will eventually need to grapple with that fact, but why hurry to such an unfortunate reality? Start by asking, "What should it be?" Envision the ideal and put off any compromises until they can no longer be avoided.

Together, these three questions, "What *could* it be?" "What *would* it be?" and "What *should* it be?" give the spark of imagination the oxygen it needs to really burn. They keep your team from getting bogged down in reality and preserve its opportunity to create. Preserving that opportunity is one of the most important facets of your job, but it can be difficult when the rest of the organization is pushing you to get real and to be more productive every day. This means that you often stand in the tension between what your organization needs to be most productive and what your team needs to be most creative, and that's a challenging place to be. Metaphorically, I picture you in the child's landscape that I described earlier. As the sky presses down to meet the ground, there is a lone figure silhouetted against the empty paper, heroically holding the two apart. That's you. It's a tough job to preserve the space to create, and some days it feels like holding up the sky.

chapter six

Opportunity to Create:

Protecting Creatives from the Fire Ants of Organizational Life

Power is no blessing in itself, except when it is used to protect the innocent.

—Jonathan Swift

MANY YEARS AGO, I was hanging out at the local playground with my daughter, and she started creating a sculpture with some small sticks she had collected. She was only four years old at the time, so I suppose it was technically more of a pile than a sculpture; but in the eyes of an adoring dad, it was a masterpiece. She was completely absorbed in it, focused entirely on the sticks in front of her and the image in her head, so she didn't realize that she had positioned her "studio" only a few feet from a fire ant hill. This was a problem. Fire ants aren't just annoying like normal ants; they are mean-spirited little cretins with no appreciation for art. They sting and have perpetually bad attitudes, so I knew that, if they discovered my daughter, there was going to be trouble.

I could've picked her up and moved to another part of the playground, but I loved how she was consumed by her project. I was eager to see how it would turn out, so I decided to become her protector instead of her relocator. I scuffed a skirmish line in the dirt between the anthill and the area where she was working, and I policed this circular band of no-man's land vigilantly. I alone stood between my daughter and the approaching horde of ants, and I vowed to rain death on any of them that dared to set feet in the bare boundary I'd made. For the next half hour, I'm sure we made an odd pair—the little girl crouching on the ground, carefully stacking sticks, and the grown man shuffling and stomping in a mad "dance of death" around her... "Take that... and that! ...You want some more of this? ...Oh, yes, that's wonderful, honey... reminiscent of Calder or Brâncuși... And that!"

I know this is a silly picture, but it's a vivid snapshot of what it means to be a protector, and when you lead a creative team, that is one of the most important roles you play. As the leader, you have one foot in the whirlwind of organizational process and productivity, and the other in the unbounded creative space of imagination and possibility. In this precarious position, it's your job to protect your team from the organizational dynamics that can take the wind out of their sails creatively or smother the fire of imagination.

Creatives are fueled by the freedom to dream, but normal organizational life has a way of surrounding them, encroaching on their mental space, and taking that freedom away. Some days, it feels like they're under siege by deadlines, work orders, and other minutia massing at

---

Creatives are fueled
by the *freedom*
to dream.

the gates. It's your job to protect your team from these and other things that can dampen their creative fire, damage their process, or distract them from their work. Like me on the playground, you need to create your own boundary and be vigilant to keep certain aspects of the work experience from getting to your team. Criticism, politics, time pressure, and boredom are some of the fire ants of organizational life that you should step on.

Criticism

Criticism is a natural part of organizational life. It comes up any time people pool their time and talent, and it's a conspicuous ingredient of the creative process itself. You need it, and you are going to see plenty of it; but you also need to protect your people from it. Criticism can smother the flames of creativity, especially if it comes too aggressively or too early in the creative process. When ideas are new and fragile or when people are laboring in the birth of them, criticism can slam on the brakes and shut imagination down. It is more helpful later in the process when promising ideas are being polished or refined.

Watch out for organizational leaders offering feedback that is miscalibrated or mistimed for bringing out the best in your team. This can preoccupy your team members with pleasing someone or satisfying some external standard, and that does not encourage imagination and innovation. The fire of creativity always sputters under the pressure to conform.

Criticism can also make your team overly concerned with perfection, and this will also dampen its fire. When people feel the pressure to get it right every time, they worry too much about mistakes and missteps. They become wary about what they think and say. This keeps interesting-but-imperfect ideas off the table, and only the safe bets and sure things get explored. That's counterproductive because extraordinary creative achievements don't usually come out of the gate looking that way. Ed Catmull, president of Pixar Animation Studios and Walt Disney Animation Studios, affirms this in stark terms, "...because early on, *all* of our movies suck... I'm not trying to be modest or self-effacing by saying this. Pixar films are not good at first, and our job is to make them so—to go, as I say, "from suck to not-suck."[1]

Great ideas, whether they are hatched at Pixar or in your own team, begin as ugly ducklings and need steady refinement to become swans. If your team feels the pressure to start with swans, you'll find that the creative fire goes out and that your dreamers are slowly replaced with editors and proofreaders. Be vigilant for discouraging comments and criticism at the wrong times. Protect fragile notions and new directions from the battering of final expectations.

Politics

Politics in your organization can threaten your team, too, and creatives need you to protect them from the negative impacts. Political maneuvering is an inescapable part of human collaboration, whether it takes place in Silicon Valley or on *Survivor*, in the legislature or *Lord of the Flies*. Any time you assemble a team and put it to work, private agendas emerge, coalitions develop, and participants jockey for credibility and influence. It's part of the way we make decisions, determine directions, and occasionally decide who to vote off the island.

But politics can negatively impact the quality of creative work, because it shifts the focus from the product to the people or agendas it should please. This takes your team's eye off the prize, and the resulting infighting, politicking, and gossip become more consuming than the quest for creative content. They get cliquish and pay more attention to navigating the political environment than to doing great work.

Politics and creativity simply don't play well together, because politics is an economy that revolves around compromise, and compromise is a lousy method for producing high-caliber creative content. Compromise pursues consensus by smoothing the edges and rounding the corners of ideas to make them the most palatable to the most people. That's not a recipe for breaking new ground, making a statement, or leading anyone in a new direction. It's a recipe for stasis. Creativity is often radical and defies consensus. It points boldly in new directions and sets the next standard instead of affirming old ones.

There are always compromises to be made as you pursue a vision, but they are best made in pursuit of excellence and the service of quality, not consensus. When you compromise simply to curry favor, you may please VIPs at the expense of the inspiring results your team initially envisioned. Politics tells creatives their work is threatened by the agendas of others and encourages them to reroute their creative energy unproductively. They can become preoccupied with manipulating those agendas or hiding their own.

To keep the fire in your team, protect it from the politics that push and pull the decisions in the organization beyond it. Strive to build a meritocracy of ideas where creatives can be sure their visions will be vetted on their own merits, not on an executive's personal color preference, a trade-off with another department, or the fact that another voice is hipper or hotter at the moment. Manage your own voice and credibility in the organization so that you can play politics on your team's behalf and protect it from the spin.

Time Pressures

Time pressure in your organization is one of the biggest threats to creativity because looming deadlines will cause your team to shorten its creative process. When the clock is ticking too loudly, your team will always settle for the safest bet, and that is seldom something extraordinary. It's usually something that's been done before or a solution that will suffice even if it won't inspire. There's not enough time for dreaming, so imagination gets reframed as a luxury or a distraction. Ideas must be born fully developed and actionable. Creatives start feeling unfulfilled because there is no time for imperfection, let alone revision and abstraction. Necessity is still the mother of invention, so the pressure of a short time frame can occasionally spur people to new achievements, but that productivity comes at a price. Perpetual urgency works against extraordinary results because it requires compromises in quality. It leads people to miss excellence by one of two routes. They either stick to previous ideas that are "sure things" from the start, or they impulsively execute new ideas that have not been adequately tested or refined. Neither route is optimal. The first trades innovation for feasibility, and the second achieves innovation at the expense of effectiveness. If you don't give creatives enough time to dream, to explore, or to take a wild goose chase or two, you won't get everything they have to offer. Unrealistic deadlines might motivate a person to move more quickly, but only to unimpressive results or to their next position in another organization.

If you want your team to do extraordinary things, then you need to protect them from unrealistic time pressures and buy them the time to do it. Your organization may not value the things your team needs, but it doesn't know what makes creatives tick (or tock) like you do. Don't let its expectations and arbitrary time-frames victimize your process or usurp your role as manager of your team. Push back against capricious or poorly considered organizational deadlines. Anticipate them or get ahead of them enough to structure your own deadlines more effectively. Hone your own planning skills so you can protect your people and give them room to breathe. They need that oxygen to stay fired up. Borrow time from the projects that can afford it, so you will have more to spend on the ones that can't.

There will inevitably be situations where time cannot be tamed, but you can make these as few and as far between as possible. In those instances, you can still manage your attitude and behavior to relieve your team's stress and to give the impression of time even when it is lacking.

Boredom

Creatives enjoy any opportunity to use their specific talents and technical skills, but they find even greater joy and fulfillment when they can do this in the service of an inspiring project. They see their work not only as the evidence of their expertise but also as an expression of themselves. This means that they are fired up by the chance to create a personal masterpiece, whether it is a pile of sticks on the playground or the ceiling of a chapel in Rome. It also means that their fire burns low at the prospect of uninspired execution. When a project exercises their technical abilities but fails to engage their imaginations, creatives get bored. They lose their enthusiasm and often their creative edge.

Unfortunately, not every project is a master-piece-in-waiting. Organizations turn to creatives for many things, and some of them are uninspiring and pedestrian. In these cases, the organization isn't looking for a creative epiphany from its internal Studio d'Art. It just needs some quick typography for the committee report, a new graph for a PowerPoint slide, or a video reminding people to turn off their phones. Can your team make this happen? Of course. Will creatives be lining up for the opportunity? Probably not. It's not the kind of thing that fans their flames. Your job is to get these things done, but to protect your team from the dulling effect of being a simple service bureau.

You can protect them from boredom and keep them fired up by managing their load more strategically. When creatives are coming off an imaginative high, they have the inspirational reserves to knock out technical tasks that don't fire them up. So try to limit or batch uninspiring projects and address them between more inspiring ones. If your team's had too much execution without inspiration lately, then you need to create opportunities for it to exercise its imaginative capacity and stay in shape creatively. Manage their expectations as well as the work. When a project offers little opportunity for creativity and requires quick execution, make sure they know it up front. Otherwise, they may try to make more of it than is necessary or desired, and this always leads to frustration and discouragement. Do your team a favor by clarifying where their imagination is best spent and best saved. I have a friend who refers to execution-without-inspiration assignments as "GEICO Projects." For years, GEICO's commercials have claimed that "15 minutes or less could save you 15%..." So he uses this label to identify any projects that are supposed to be "quickies," the ones that should require minimal time and effort for the designer completing it. In the lexicon of his department, this helps creatives manage their time, but, more importantly, it right-sizes their expectations so they can allocate their personal investment more realistically. He makes sure that no one on his team has a steady diet of "GEICO Projects" and that he is disbursing them in the midst of more inspiring work. In this way, he serves his organization's needs, but he also protects his team from the boredom that can dampen its fire over time.

That's the challenge of your role, too, if you lead a creative team in the midst of a not-so-creative organization. An organization's nature and needs aren't always conducive to kindling or keeping a fire in your team. The dynamics that drive these organizations can suck the air out of creatives and suffocate imagination. This means that you need to surround them with an oxygenated bubble in which they can burn. You're the crazy father on the playground protecting the opportunity to create. You're their defender, their protector, their stomper-of-ants.

FUEL

WHEN I WAS young, we heated our house with wood. This meant that I spent a good portion of every autumn helping my father cut firewood for the winter. I learned that certain kinds of wood were preferable to others because they made a better fire. Pine and poplar were dirty and burned up quickly. Oak and hickory were hot and lasted a long time. Cedar would spit sparks on your carpet and make your mom mad. You had to have the right fuel if you wanted to keep a good fire going in the stove.

It's not so different when you are trying to kindle and keep a fire burning in your team. Every fire needs to be fed, and you need the right fuel. Without it, the spark of imagination will simply flash and disappear. You can keep adding heat and oxygen, but without sufficient fuel, you'll never get it to burn. You'll just create the kind of hot and hungry environment that devours everyone involved.

The powerful transformation that produces light and energy is consuming, and so is the creative process. Creatives need fuel to keep going, or they will quickly burn up or burn out. If you want to keep them fired up, you've got to do more than turn up the heat and give them room to breathe; you've got to stoke the fire in their bellies.

The chapters in this section encourage you to drive out fear, pump up the purpose, share the power, build trust, and have fun so your team won't run out of fuel.

OXYGEN HEAT

FUEL

chapter seven

Freedom from Fear:

Diagnosing the Fear Factor &
Dogs that Won't Hunt

*People won't remember what you say, or what you do, but they will
remember how you make them feel.*

—Maya Angelou

RECENTLY, A FRIEND complained to me about the performance of his hunting dog. As an "upland" hunter,
he relied on the dog to find quail, pheasants, and other
birds hidden in the brush, to point them out and to retrieve them after his shot. I asked him what the dog was
doing—Ignoring commands? Flushing birds? Failing to
retrieve? His response surprised me... "Nothing," he
said. "She's doing absolutely nothing. She just lies down
and won't hunt at all." I found this intriguing and asked
him to join me for a hunt.

He arrived at the field with a good-looking English
Setter in the back of his pickup truck. She was excited
and seemed to have much more pep in her step than
he had described. In fact, she jumped out of the truck
before it stopped, ears up and tail wagging, but an odd
thing happened when he put an e-collar on her.

An e-collar, or electronic collar, is a dog-training device that delivers a small shock when a button is pushed on a remote transmitter. The shock is uncomfortable, but not painful. (I've tried it on myself to be sure.) You can adjust the intensity of it with the remote, so it provides metered and immediate feedback from a distance. Think of an e-collar as a leash that you can tug from across a field.

When the hunter buckled the e-collar on his dog and said, "Let's go!" the dog's demeanor changed dramatically. The perkiness vanished, and she stood stiff-legged and wide-eyed as he alternately commanded and begged her to hunt. She wouldn't even look at him. To my surprise, he even shocked her a couple of times as a sort of punctuation to his pleas, but she still stood motionless and miserable. He looked at me, defeated, and said, "See what I mean?" I said, "Yeah, it looks like she's not too keen on hunting today, or maybe she doesn't understand what you want."

"Oh, she knows what I want," he said. "I practice with her all the time... C'mon, get up!" With his exclamation, he brandished the remote and shocked her again. I'm not sure what he thought this would do, but he was clearly defeated when the dog simply lay down on the ground and looked away. "I just don't get it," he said. "She used to be excited about hunting, but it seems like the more we work on it, the worse she gets. Can you fix her?"

"I'm not sure she's broken," I answered, "but I think we can improve things a little. Let's start with this..." and I bent down to remove the e-collar from his dog.

Follow the Leader

It's a funny thing about dogs—and people. They follow the leader more than you think. I suppose there are some ornery individuals that are lost causes from the start, but I find them pretty rare in both dogs and people. More often, I discover that poor performers aren't broken, and the problems or failures attributed to them are more accurately placed on the shoulders of those in authority over them.

In these cases, "fixing things" means changing the leader. My friend's dog wasn't the problem. It was my friend's finger on the shock button that was demotivating the dog and damaging her performance. In fact, it appeared that he'd shocked her so much that the shock no longer had much effect at all. If you are trying to kindle and keep the fire burning in your team, then you can learn a lot from my friend.

Fear is an especially powerful motivator, but its ability to compel behavior in the short run often distracts people from the negative impact it has over time. Fear doesn't fuel people; it depletes them. In the long run, its animating effect is reversed. It eventually dampens emotional, intellectual, and physical activity and shuts everything down.

Fear is also desensitizing. This means that the more you use it, more of it is needed to produce the same effect over time. That's why leaders who motivate with fear often find themselves unconsciously upping the ante and accelerating the demise of their teams. I worked for a boss like this who reminded me that my job hung in the balance with each assignment he gave. I needed the job, so naturally, the prospect of losing it motivated me to give my best effort; and I stepped up my game. But eventually, after repeatedly facing the prospect of being fired, I grew weary of worrying. I was just tired of being afraid. My boss seemed to sense this and redoubled his threats to regain my attention. This only increased my "fear fatigue" until one day when he threatened to fire me, all I could think was, "Fine. Go ahead."

You might think that too much fear would eventually prompt agitation or aggression, and it might, but not for very long. Any fire fear kindles in someone burns out quickly because, when fear becomes too prevalent, it shuts them down. It creates a "damned-if-you-do-and-damned-if-you-don't" reality where passivity, apathy, and inactivity seem like the best options. When people believe that any choice or move they make will produce a negative response, they try to make as few of them as possible. They become increasingly passive, unproductive, and surprisingly unresponsive to the same fear that motivated them initially. Put more simply, they don't rise up; they lie down.

——

When people believe
that any choice or move
they make will produce
a negative response,
they try to make as few
of them as possible.

The psychological principle behind this is called learned helplessness, and it threatens creatives and creative teams as much as it does hunting dogs. If the members of your team are more worried about getting in trouble or covering their backsides than about advancing the mission or doing great work, creativity (and quality in general) becomes irrelevant. Self-preservation becomes their mission instead, and the team's best move, like my friend's dog, is to cease moving at all.

When learned helplessness characterizes a team's behavior, it initiates a slow and silent death. The fire in the team dwindles and dies as the inspiration and hope that fuel it disappear. It's not a flashy thing, so you may not notice that it's happening at first. Chronic or cultural fear doesn't detonate or tear a team apart; it debilitates it, cripples it, and calcifies it until it simply stops.

To borrow imagery from Robert Frost, some teams perish in fire and some in ice. Some flare out magnificently, crashing and burning in the conflagration of massive miscalculations, market shifts, or moral meltdowns. But more are extinguished quietly, frozen in inactivity or irrelevance as the rest of the world moves on, and competitors step over their cool remains. Fear can contribute to either of these demises, but it is most frequently responsible for the latter.

Effects of Fear

You need to be especially wary of fear in your team, because it makes the members smaller and less capable than they actually are. It puts a lid on creatives' performance and imagination and robs you of the fuel you need to get the job done. Take a moment to audit your own team's dynamics for the following four signs that fear is limiting its potential.

NEGATIVE COMPETITION AND DIMINISHED TRUST. When there is too much fear, people prioritize their own safety above everything else. Relying on others becomes too risky, and vulnerability grows scarce. As a result, team members can't build trust, and some may even protect or advance themselves at the expense others. It's like the well-worn joke about two hunters who spot a hungry grizzly bear heading for their camp. As it closes in, one hunter starts changing his boots for running shoes, and his companion says, "What are you doing? You can't outrun that bear." The first hunter replies, "I don't need to; I only need to outrun *you*."

SHORT-TERM THINKING. Fear focuses people on the here and now. This is probably a good strategy in the face of that hungry grizzly, but it's less useful when you're a member of a creative team. In this environment, it's often your ability to look beyond the present that distinguishes you and your work. Fear fosters a climate where this is less pertinent. Longer-term issues and implications are eclipsed by immediate threats. As a result, your team may find itself regularly rethinking, redoing, or cleaning up messes it's made for itself. **LACK OF INNOVATION.** Nothing feels the negative impact of fear faster than creativity. Remember, when a team is afraid to make the wrong move, they won't move at all. The risk of extending themselves physically, cognitively, or emotionally into the unknown dissuades them from thinking new thoughts, let alone exploring unproven or uncertain paths. The status quo gets too sticky, and the team's ideas and imagination seldom stray far from it. Ironically, this determination to avoid failure virtually guarantees it, because it leads individuals and organizations to resist the risks prerequisite to any success.

LACK OF JOY OR PRIDE IN THE WORK. Fear not only grounds a team's dreams, but it also stifles the joy that might come from enacting them. When projects feel more like maneuvers to manage risk or mitigate negative consequences than opportunities to create or advance something new, the joy disappears. Creatives are inherently generative people, and it's tough for them to be proud and fulfilled by experiences that feel defensive or remediating.

Stopping Fear at its Source

If any of these things sound familiar to you, then fear may be dampening spirits and keeping your team from catching fire. If you want to fuel your creatives' fire, you need to drive it out of their experience wherever you find it. Here are three of the best places to look[2]:

1. Abusive Conduct

Any aggressive interpersonal behavior that intimidates, demeans, humiliates, or isolates people creates fear in a team. This means that you should avoid the obvious misbehaviors of threats, insults, shouting, or emotional outbursts in your interactions with creatives. There is certainly a place for fiery leadership. A passionate, demonstrative leader can fire up team members and inspire more emotional commitment to the work, but an angry, abrasive, and volatile one will shut them down fast. That kind of aggressiveness makes creatives regret and resist the vulnerability that creating requires.

Fear is also produced by less combative behavior, like silence, pointed eye contact, brevity, abruptness, or simply ignoring people. These behaviors are quieter and often unintentional but still abusive. They're harder to recognize in the moment, but they are just as detrimental to your team. They distance and demean and keep people from investing themselves in what they're doing. If you want creatives to be brave and at their best, then you need to confront and eliminate abusive behavior wherever you see it. Not simply because it is unkind or unappealing, but because it is unproductive and it siphons off the fuel your team needs to burn brightly.

Spend some time thinking about abusive behavior and the ways you see it cropping up in your team's interactions. If you're really brave, ask your team where they see it cropping up in yours. Then commit yourself to driving it out. Don't tolerate it or think it's just a passing thing. It's stealing your fuel and diminishing the fire in your team.

2. Ambiguous Behavior

Abusive conduct is stark and easy to spot once you know to look for it, but other, less obvious actions (or non-actions) can be fostering fear in your team, as well. These Ambiguous Behaviors include things like ineffective problem solving and decision making, insufficient or indirect communication, unresponsiveness, unfinished business, unresolved questions, inconsistency, and mixed messages. "Loose ends" like these create anxiety in your team because they are difficult to "read." They make expectations and direction unclear and de-fuel your creatives. They are also embarrassingly common because ambiguity is hard to avoid in the dynamic environment and accelerated pace of most organizations.

I know your organization isn't tidy, so eliminating ambiguity altogether is probably not an option. Instead, make it your goal to distinguish yourself and your sphere of influence as a source of clarity in the midst of everything else. In this case, diminishing fear and fueling your team isn't about eliminating all of the unknowns; it's about reliably bringing order out of the chaos.

Ironically, when things are at their messiest, they're most ambiguous, your greatest contribution may not lie in cleaning it up, but in simply clarifying the mess. Leaders frequently overlook the importance of naming the "elephant in the room" or of acknowledging the loose ends and questions in people's minds when they are not prepared to resolve them. Leaving these things unspoken maximizes anxiety because it isolates your team members and leaves them wondering if anyone else shares their concerns. If you can resolve questions and concerns, you should. If you can't, then naming the questions and articulating a process to resolve them eventually is still a strong step in the right direction. It gives your team the confidence that you are paying attention, and it drives their fear away.

If you want to fuel the fire in your team, then focus on being responsive and communicative. Create clarity where you can, acknowledge the ambiguity where you can't, and steadily, collaboratively, move forward in the mess.

3. Poor Personnel Management

The previous two sections described behaviors to minimize if you want to reduce fear and fuel your team. This section identifies a context that merits special attention: Personnel Management. Research and experience identify that the way you handle personnel and performance issues is especially potent in producing or diminishing fear in your team. Team members pay a lot of attention to decisions about hiring, termination, and performance. They're not just watching; they are extrapolating and applying what they observe to their own experience. They say to themselves, "If that happened to so-and-so, it could happen to me!" So a situation handled poorly with one person can produce worry and anxiety in many more. To drive out this fear, you not only need to make good decisions and demonstrate courage and compassion to whoever is directly involved, but you also need to manage the message it conveys to everyone who is not involved. This can be tricky because of the confidentiality that surrounds such matters.

Observers rarely know the backstories behind what they see, but they are inclined to assume the worst. Lacking real details, they invent their own, and they tend to do so in the ways they find most frightening. For this reason, complete silence on personnel actions may not be your best strategy for minimizing fear, especially if yours is a small team where the action is most visible and the grapevine is most active. It's inappropriate to broadcast the specific details of your decisions to the wider audience, but it may be wise to address the specific fears they could fuel.

For example, an employee's termination may seem sudden to those who are not involved in the decision, even if the situation has been brewing for months. They may assume that the action was unexpected and fear that they too could be disciplined or dismissed without warning. In sensitive matters like this, you aren't able to say much about what the situation *is*, but you can say plenty about what it *is not*. Try meeting with the team and saying something like, "As you know, we've made a decision to terminate Bill's employment here. While it would be inappropriate for me to share details of this specific situation, I want to reassure you that decisions like this are never made easily or quickly. We arrive at them only after careful consideration and communication and after multiple interactions over time." This doesn't tell people anything about the immediate event, but it speaks volumes about the process and commitment of the organization. More importantly, the message speaks directly to their fears and reassures them that they could never find themselves in a similar situation without plenty of warning, communication, and opportunity to address the issues.

If you are going to get the best out of creatives or hunting dogs, then you need to be wary and wise about fear. It's not as simple as ruling it out of your leadership repertoire altogether. In small doses, fear can escalate attention or improve initiative, and a good leader invokes it when he clarifies the importance of a goal or reminds the team what's at stake. But if you rely on these tactics too often or fail to manage the three sources of fear I've described, you will see rapidly diminishing returns. Fear will steal the hope and inspiration that fuels the fire in your team, and any motivation will be just a flash in the pan. Your creatives might burn, but only briefly before their reserves are consumed and their fire goes out. Instead, commit to driving fear out of your team. Refine your leadership and the behavior in your team so that it stokes the fire instead of sapping it. As the leader, you set the tone, so show them what it looks like to be fearless. Take the e-collar off and let them hunt.

chapter eight

Power to the People:

You're Not a Doer Anymore

Even though capacity and motivation are destroyed when leaders choose power over productivity, it appears that bosses would rather be in control than have the organization work well.

—Margaret J. Wheatley

IF YOU ARE a Leader now, I'll wager you were an excellent Doer earlier in your career. That's the way it usually works. You distinguished yourself as a person who can do certain tasks and deliver certain outcomes personally. Your technical expertise, your work ethic, and your ability to roll up your sleeves and get the job done all helped you to stand out from the crowd. Your reward was a promotion, and you became a supervisor, a manager, or a leader. Congratulations!

This move from Doer to Leader is one of the toughest transitions to make in your career because it's a complete paradigm shift, and no one tells you it's coming. A leadership or management role isn't just the next rung on the ladder or the same job you've been doing pitched bigger and higher. It's a different job altogether, and you might be surprised to find that many of the inclinations that distinguished you as a Doer are no longer as useful to you as a Leader. In fact, some of your go-to Doer habits turn out to be liabilities in leadership because Doers and Leaders need to have very different dispositions toward power and what to do with it.

Great Doers focus directly on the outcomes and it's this focus that inspires them to do whatever it takes to achieve the goal.

Figure 8.1

In a leadership role, however, this same focus on the outcome can be problematic because there are other people involved. It's no longer just you and the goal; there are team members to consider. Leaders that fail to realize this difference and adjust their focus, end up ignoring their teams or viewing them as troubling complications or impediments between them and the goals they are trying to achieve.

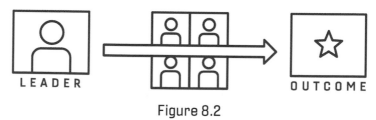

Figure 8.2

Great Leaders focus on their teams. They are not unaware or unconcerned about outcomes, but they realize that they will not be able to achieve them in their own power. So, they turn their attention to empowering the people they lead.

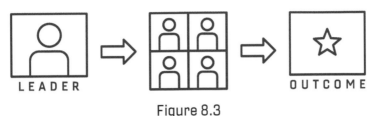

Figure 8.3

Think of it this way: Great Doers are distinguished by their *direct* achievements, their ability to personally take the ball and run with it. So, they tend to be oriented more toward personal performance than stoking the fire in others. They amass power for their own use, roll up their sleeves, and get busy. Great Leaders are distinguished by their *indirect* achievements, their ability to give the ball to someone else and help them run well. So, they focus on their people and build team members' power and inclination to use it.

When you are a Leader, the things your team is charged to create or deliver are going to be accomplished directly by the Doers but indirectly by you. If all goes well, your greatest creations will have the fingerprints of your creatives all over them, but not your own. Of course, you'll make vital contributions, but they will be one step removed from the final product. Your mark will be on the Doers.

In practice, especially in smaller, more collaborative teams, the distinction between Leaders and Doers gets blurred. I describe the difference sharply here for clarity's sake and to encourage you to think of it this way. In my experience, Leaders who do not envision their roles very differently than those of Doers, wind up confusing and competing with the people they lead. They inadvertently create dependencies instead of opportunities and become the limiters of their teams' talents and capacity. Alternatively, Leaders who recast themselves and rework the habits they learned as Doers fuel the potential of their people and fan the flames of their teams.

You create potent, independent contributors and a team that transcends the sum of its parts when you resist doing and instead invest in the Doers. If the product is lacking, your first move shouldn't be to improve it yourself. It should be to prepare, motivate, or direct one of your team members to improve it instead. This shift of focus is important because creatives are intrinsically motivated and need to feel potent in order to stay engaged and productive. They need to feel powerful enough to incarnate the visions in their heads, to make choices, and to change the trajectory of their projects. If they do not feel like they have this power, or there are too many constraints on it, they will run out of gas. They'll begin to feel like the practical and emotional investments of creating won't be worth the effort, and their creative pilot light will go out.

To prevent this, you need to keep creatives fueled with the sense of power and potency they need to keep burning bright. This can be difficult if you are still a Doer at heart, because your older instincts will steer you wrong. They will lead you to do too much yourself and leave the Doers feeling left out or low on fuel. Here are three counterintuitive strategies to help you shift from Doer to Leader and keep the power with your people.

Differences between Doers and Leaders:

Doers	Leaders
Focus directly on the outcome	Focus directly on the people
Take Control	Give Control
Amass Knowledge	Share Knowledge
Exert Influence	Give Influence
Take Responsibility	Assign Responsibility
Elevate Personal Engagement	Elevate Others' Engagement
Effectiveness is demonstrated by impacting the Outcome. Your own ability to achieve the outcome.	Effectiveness is demonstrated by impacting the People. Others' ability to achieve the outcome.

Figure 8.4

Stop doing what needs to be done

When people first step into leadership, they expect it to be hard, but they often have the wrong idea of why. They still think in Doer terms and anticipate that the weight of what needs to be done will be heavier in a higher role. It turns out that the hardest part of leading is not the doing, but the not doing. When you are accustomed to doing things yourself, it's difficult to direct others to do them instead. It's hard to tell them what to do and even harder to wait for their results. But if you want to fuel your team with the power to do great things, you must resist the temptation of doing those things yourself.

If you are a compassionate leader and it's difficult for you to ask others to do things, I can relate. It's far more comfortable for me to "up" my own game or work harder myself than to ask my people to up theirs. But that's what exceptional leaders do. They inspire greater commitment and contribution from their teams, and that's never going to happen if you are providing those things yourself. When you need to ask others to step up to a challenge, remind yourself that you are actually giving them the chance to feel powerful. Try not to think of your request as an imposition as much as an opportunity.

When you were a Doer yourself, and you went the extra mile, did the extra work, stayed after hours, etc., you might not have enjoyed it in the moment; but you probably felt a certain satisfaction in being strong enough or capable enough to do it. It felt good to be the hero and demonstrate your commitment to the cause. Some of these moments eventually became your personal badges of honor. Now, when similar moments arise, try to remember that they are your team members' moments, not yours. Don't step in and steal their opportunities to shine.

Leaders in creative organizations have often risen up from the ranks. This means that they are often card-carrying creatives themselves. You know what needs to be done and have the ability to get it done yourself, but don't. You're not a Doer anymore. If you roll up your sleeves and get busy, you're usually taking that opportunity away from someone else. If you do too much to affect the outcomes directly, your team members will quickly feel unnecessary, frustrated, or demeaned. Your good intentions and high standards won't save you, because the problem isn't your aspirations. It's your inability to trust others with the responsibility of achieving them. So resist the urge to do things yourself in the interest of powering-up your people. Fuel their contribution instead of firing up your own.

As I write these words, I can feel you struggling with an internal tension and asking, "Wait a minute. Aren't leaders supposed to model the behavior they desire? When the moment calls for people to demonstrate their commitment, shouldn't the leader demonstrate his or hers?" The answer is an emphatic, "Yes!" But *what* you model and *how* you demonstrate your commitment makes a difference.

Leaders and Doers demonstrate commitment differently. Doers demonstrate commitment by turning up the time and attention they give to the work. Leaders do it by turning up the time and attention they give the Doers. Doers want their Leaders to be aware and appreciative of their contributions, but they don't want Leaders to do the work for them. This means that you need to be able to demonstrate that you are in the fray with them without making them feel incidental.

I learned a powerful lesson in this several years ago when one of my own teams was headed into the final stretch of a lengthy project and discovered an error that needed to be fixed. It was the kind of error that I almost wished we hadn't found, because fixing it would require massive revisions and a very late and stressful night for everyone. The Doer in me was about to declare "all hands on deck" and dive in to the rework personally, but as I was about to do this, one of the team leaders came into my office and told me they had scrapped the current production and scheduled the staff to work through the night. "We got this," she said. I swallowed the voice of my inner Doer as it rose in my throat and simply said, "Thank you. I know it's going to be a long night."

I'd like to say that I did this because I was a sophisticated leader who appreciated the nuances of empowering my people, but the truth is there was something about the way she said, "We got this," that also said, "Leave us alone." The look in her eye told me this was a leader and a team that felt powerful enough to do whatever it took to complete their mission. I needed the reminder. In this moment of truth, being a good leader wasn't about providing my assistance as much as giving my respect and support. If I tried to step in, I'd only be meddling or making them feel smaller.

So I went home at the end of the workday and left the team hard at work. It wasn't easy. My inner Doer felt guilty and complained the whole way, but I had a plan. At midnight, I returned to the office with the most meaningful contribution I could make—a stack of pizzas and an extra generous helping of good humor and gratitude. I only stayed for a short time, just long enough to share a slice and pat some backs, and then I went home to bed and left the heroes to their work.

This is my point: Leaders should model the way, and in this case that meant demonstrating the commitment to go above and beyond. But the way a Leader goes above and beyond isn't always the same as a Doer. My late night pizza delivery modeled my attentiveness and willingness to participate in the rescue effort, but it didn't communicate doubts or usurp the power of the team. In the end, the project came out great and error-free, but, more importantly, the team emerged from the experience more potent than ever. They wore their fatigue as a badge of honor and were empowered by the ordeal.

It turns out that fueling the fire in your team often requires you to do less than you think, much less. You steal people's power when you do too much yourself, and you can make them stronger by staying out of it and offering encouragement (and a slice of pizza) along the way.

Stop answering questions

When you are a Doer, your path to greater influence and opportunity lies in your ability to provide the answers. You might do this literally, by providing the data or information that decision-makers require, or metaphorically, by providing the solution to new problems and opportunities that arise. Either way, your ability to personally provide answers is the key to your credibility, the measure of your effectiveness, and your ticket to the "big time." However, once you've made it to the "big time" and you're leading a team yourself, your ability or inclination to provide the answers is not only less useful, it's counterproductive. It fails to fuel your team and makes it hard for them to stay fired up.

As a leader, your success doesn't come from how much you know; it comes from how much your people know. You need them to provide the answers, and they tend not to do this if you are busily doing it yourself. A frustrated leader recently complained to me that her people would not "step up and answer the tough questions." She found this lack of knowledge and initiative inexplicable. "When I was in their position," she said, "I always had the answers." I believe her. She probably did have the answers, but part of her problem was that she still did. If she wants her people to take more initiative in making choices and answering questions themselves, then she needs to get out of the way and make more space for them to do it.

You might need to do the same. Creatives will adjust their behavior to yours, so if you are too full of answers, then you will eventually discover that they are too full of questions. They will increasingly pass the critical choices on to you and wait for your direction. This slows everything down and shifts the power unproductively away from the ones who need to be exercising it most. In short order, you will feel like your team moves only when you do.

The problem here isn't really a lack of initiative; it's a lack of power. The team needs fuel. So pump up your team's power by flipping the script. Stop answering questions and start asking them instead. Audit your e-mails for sufficient question marks before you hit "send." Let people leave your office without answers more often. This doesn't mean that you should stop offering feedback and guidance altogether—being clueless and disengaged isn't a great strategy for either Leaders or Doers—but tailor your guidance to shape others' consideration. Give the kind of assistance that empowers them to find answers themselves.

When I was young and asked my parents what a word meant, they always told me to look in the dictionary. How frustrating! It would've been much easier if they had simply given me an answer, but now I realize they were giving me power instead. Their response gave me the incentive and ability to meet my own needs instead of fostering a dependence on them. I'm not sure my younger self would buy this, but I think of it now when I fuel my team by offering resources, contacts, and food for thought instead of answers.

By the way, when your people have questions, I know you know the answers. They might even be better ones than others would provide, but you should still resist giving them. When you're the Leader, getting the best answer isn't your only concern. You're also trying to build a powerful team and fuel your people with the confidence and inclination to seek their own answers. To this end, it's sometimes better to have a lesser answer, as long as it comes from someone else. When you already know the answer, it can be hard to wait for one from someone else, but sometimes speed isn't what you need most, either. When what you need most is a team that is fired up and producing great answers for itself, your silence and patience are some of the best fuel you can provide.

Risk more of your reputation on someone else's work

It is especially difficult to empower other people with things like your own inactivity and silence when your reputation rests on the quality of their work. When you were a Doer, your own work represented you for better or for worse. It might've been stressful, but it was a fairly empowered position to be in. Now that you are a Leader, your credibility is vested in someone else's work, and you rise and fall on what they do. This is a more vulnerable position, and it makes the shift in power that fuels your team simultaneously more important and more frightening. It's tempting to protect yourself by limiting your team's ability to make choices that might reflect poorly on your own reputation. Leaders do this consciously and subconsciously in the ways they shape projects and delegate authority, but either way it limits their teams' power and fails to fuel the fire they need.

As a general rule, if you feel safe and are confident that the efforts of your people can't harm your reputation, then you've probably not given them enough power. You've either given them sham choices where you've hedged your bets and given them only enough latitude to make choices that don't make much difference, or you've created a situation where the team is just an extension of your own imagination, judgment, and preferences. These tactics make you feel safer because they allow you to remain the master of your own reputation, but they are also limiting. They leave your team incapable of transcending your personal limits and leave creatives feeling claustrophobic.

Instead, risk your rep on your team. Give it room to work and real choices to make. Draw the boundaries for their ideas and the latitude for their decisions wide enough for creatives to feel empowered rather than constrained. This is likely to make you nervous because your sense of control usually diminishes as theirs increases, but resist the urge to tighten up. Control is overrated; it limits even more than it protects. Ease your discomfort by supporting the players and the process.

You fuel them when you shape the values and goals that guide their use of power, rather than limiting their access to it altogether.

Ultimately, the shift from Doer to Leader is difficult because it feels like you are giving power away. You are—that's what you do when you're trying to fuel other people—but this doesn't make you weaker. When you make the transition from doing into leading, you need to adjust how you conceptualize power, not simply how you exercise it. The new realities may confound any Doer sensibilities that persist because they sound a little crazy from a Doer's point of view. As a Leader, you are weakest when you lean on your own sufficiency, and you grow more powerful only when you give power away. That's the paradox at the heart of great leadership. When you stop doing what needs to be done, stop answering questions, and risk more on the efforts of others, you are actually firing up your team. When you fuel their success, you're fostering your own.

chapter nine

Fun:

Using Humor and Play to Improve Innovation, Collaboration, and Stamina

There is little success where there is little laughter.

—Andrew Carnegie

In Dante's Inferno, the sign that hung over the gates of Hell read, "Abandon Hope All Ye Who Enter Here." Sometimes I find myself looking for a similar sign at the entrance of offices and workspaces. One that reads, "Abandon *Fun* All Ye Who Enter Here," because these thresholds seem to mark the descent into a hell of focused productivity where all lightness and levity are left behind.

Candidly, when I first wrote the previous paragraph, I thought it was too dramatic, too extreme—who quotes Dante in a leadership book? But the following day, as I stood in the lobby of a corporate headquarters, I changed my mind. It was spot on. I watched a steady stream of people arriving to start their workday, and as they passed the security desk, they seemed to check their fun at the door. I'm convinced the officer wasn't there to let the employees in as much as he was there to keep any levity out!

One woman came into the lobby laughing loudly and talking animatedly on her phone, but as she neared the security desk she said soberly into it, "Gotta go. Time to put on my game face and get to work." She hung up and composed herself to step up to the gate. The transformation was startling. She changed from an animated, bright, and expressive woman into a buttoned-down, poker-faced, dialed-back, and dimmed down version of herself just in time to pass through security and board the elevator. If this was the game face, I could only conclude that the game was no fun at all!

The sad truth is that many of us make similar transformations when we go to work. We compose ourselves to be appropriately focused, serious, and "on task." After all, it *is* work, and that's serious business, right? There's no room for fun in the land where productivity is king. Or is there?

Research and experience affirm that it's possible to be so "on task" that your overall productivity suffers, especially when creativity is required. The old adage "All work and no play, makes Jack a dull boy" proves too true. Stuart Brown, author of *Play: How it Shapes the Brain, Opens the Imagination, and Invigorates the Soul*, concluded after following over 6000 individuals:

> Play-deprived adults are often rigid, humorless, inflexible and closed to trying out new options.

Playfulness enhances the capacity to innovate, adapt and master changing circumstances. It is not just an escape. It can help us integrate and reconcile difficult or contradictory circumstances. And, often, it can show us a way out of our problems.[3]

Conventional wisdom encourages leaders to eliminate distractions and keep their teams on task to get the most out of them, but that's not always best. If you want to fuel the fire in creatives, you often need to lighten up, not tighten up. In today's idea and intelligence economy, productivity depends on innovation, collaboration, and stamina as much as focus; and increasing the humor and playfulness in your team can foster them all.

Innovation

Success in most creative endeavors turns on your team's ability and inclination to think outside the box, but when an environment is too rigid or rules-bound, creatives spend more time paying attention to the box than thinking outside it. Humor and play fuel innovation by loosening the constraints of mental boundaries and encouraging people to entertain fresh ideas, unexpected connections, and new directions. They create space where conventional expectations are suspended for a while. That's how comedians can say the things you aren't *supposed* to say and how games allow us to explore implausible scenarios or compete without the consequences of "real life" contention.

In the composed arenas of humor and play, we are able to think and do unusual things precisely because we aren't held back by the usual ones. The normal rules don't apply, at least not in the same ways, so we often find ourselves in new or unexpected places. It's like the Loony Tunes cartoon from the 1940s where Bugs Bunny is chased off the edge of a cliff by a hunter but doesn't fall. He just stands there magically suspended in midair, munching his carrot. The hunter tells him this is impossible because of the law of gravity, and Bugs explains, "I never studied law." When your people laugh or engage in playful interactions, some of the usual laws that constrain them become irrelevant, and they can imagine and do things that would have been impossible before. When innovation matters, fun fuels the creative engine and fires up your team.

Collaboration

Collaboration is another hallmark of successful creative teams that is fostered well with fun. Your team members may be talented individuals, but together they're even better. If you want to get the most out of them, then you need them to combine their talents and imagination to become better than any of them are independently. This kind of interdependence depends on

If you want to fuel the
fire in creatives, you
often need to *lighten up*,
not *tighten up*.

the team members' ability to trust and be vulnerable with each other. Having fun together breaks down the walls that distance people and inhibit trust.

When people are in "work mode," they are hyper-vigilant about what is expected of them, and they manage their interactions and relationships carefully to conform to it. They compose themselves to be appropriate, like the woman on the phone I mentioned earlier. This isn't a bad habit overall, especially if they work in an environment where professionalism and decorum are important, but striving for conformity isn't the best posture for developing trust, because it inhibits authenticity. When people are overly focused on being what they are supposed to be, they often fail to be who they really are. Their relationships are guarded and impersonal. They may rely on the formal contributions of teammates or the service required by their roles, but they don't really trust any of them personally. As a result, they don't practice the kind of personal vulnerability that interdependence requires. They just aren't real, and when people aren't real with one another, trust is slow to grow, and collaboration is pretty thin.

These kinds of sterilized interactions might produce a collection of politely cooperative people, but not a true team. Teams transcend the sum of their parts and are distinguished by the kind of synergy and interdependence that only comes from members' openness and vulnerability with each other. Humor and play are powerful catalysts for building this kind of strong collaboration, because a fun or funny experience takes the focus off the expectations and encourages people to be themselves.

Humor, in particular, has a special way of making people real. It comes in under their radar or around the professional barriers they've built and opens them up. That's why speakers and salespeople often begin their remarks with a joke or a humorous story. They know that, when we laugh, we are more open. We relax the guards on our hearts, and we lower the barriers that temper our relationships. We are more "real" in the sense that we are functioning at a deeper and more holistic emotional level than in more sober or professionally contrived moments.

Brain scans reveal that most emotional responses are confined to isolated areas of the brain, but our response to humor is much more complex and comprehensive.[4] It simultaneously engages multiple parts of our brains that manage things like friendship, love, and affection. This makes us especially open and relationally oriented when we laugh. We're emotionally prepared to make deeper, more personal connections with others. This means that fun may be the producer, as much as the product, of great relationships. So, next time you enjoy a good laugh with your friends, consider the possibility that you might be friends because you've enjoyed laughs like that before. Encourage your creatives to laugh, too, *because* it fuels the kind of collaborative spirit they need to stay fired up.

Stamina

If you want to fuel your team and help it to be productive, then you need to keep its fire burning over time. The rigors of work take their toll, and it's hard for creatives to stay at the top of their game when the load is high and unrelenting. They simply run out of gas, and their imagination and productivity suffers not for lack of skill, but for lack of stamina. They need some fun. When the workload is high and the prospect of decreasing it is low, fun can fuel endurance and revitalize people in ways that perks, pep talks, and overtime pay never will.

When it comes to creatives' stamina, it's not the weight of the load that matters as much as how they carry it. If they are depressed, discouraged, or fearful, they are weakened and diminished; and the load feels especially heavy. They will find it daunting to shoulder the basic responsibilities of their roles, let alone to invent new ones.

But if they are happy, they are stronger and more resilient versions of themselves. They have more to give, and they bounce back better from the setbacks and complications that come their way. So, if you want to fuel your team's strength and endurance, you should help them be happier. Play proves to be your secret weapon in this effort because it has the unique ability to draw people in to the present, and the present is the only place they can truly be happy.

One of the reasons people aren't happier in general is that they aren't very good at being present in the living of their own lives. They tend to dwell on the past and wrestle with regret, disappointment, and anger over what did or didn't happen; or they fixate on the future and grapple with the fear and anxiety of what might or might not happen. Either way, they end up emotionally distracted and fatigued by the things they can no longer affect or those that may never occur!

This tendency often leaves creatives spiritually and emotionally distant from where they are physically, and this kind of fractured experience is tiring to maintain. It erodes their endurance and smothers the fire that burns inside them. Play changes this situation and fuels that fire by centering them in the present moment. It pulls creatives' attention and emotion into the same spot as their bodies, so they can be wholly absorbed by their experience for a time. This lifts the unproductive weight of past and future worries and creates a moment of recovery that improves their endurance.

Humor can create a similar respite, but by different means. Instead of drawing people fully into their current experience, it can remove them from it altogether. Humor can't transport them physically, but it can relocate them emotionally and lighten their load by changing their perspective.

I saw this in action recently after an especially rough landing on a Southwest Airlines flight. The plane touched down suddenly, lurched to the left, veered to the right, and shuddered violently before stabilizing and continuing to taxi down the runway. Passengers were tense, knuckles were white, and the cabin was a sea of anxious and angry faces. Then the voice of the pilot came over the intercom saying, "Whooooooa! Easy there big fella..." and laughter erupted throughout the cabin. A little humor changed everything. One moment people were distracted and diminished by their fears, and the next they were relaxed and reoriented. Weighty and diminishing emotions like frustration and fear evaporated with a few well-chosen and well-timed words.

Humor helps us transcend the circumstances that might otherwise consume or constrain us and enables us to carry on. Another case in point from the airline industry, courtesy of Virgin Atlantic, illustrates this.[5] One of their planes was delayed, and the passengers in the gate area were growing increasingly impatient. As the minutes ticked by, the crowd's frustration festered until the following message came up on the screen: *"Our aircraft is arriving late due to traffic restrictions. Once the aircraft parks at the gate, a rabid badger will be released at the rear of the aircraft to encourage people to exit forward quickly. Once we have secured the badger and cleaned up the cabin, we will board."* Immediately, clenched jaws gave way to smirks.

People stopped texting the customer service department and started snapping photos of the sign, instead. The circumstances were the same. The plane was late, but the experience was altogether different in a moment.

If you want to fuel the innovation, collaboration, and stamina of your team by having more fun, consider these three tips:

1. Take the work seriously but not yourself

When you are working on important things, it's easy to let the gravity of what you're trying to do drive the fun out of the experience of doing it. So lighten up. You don't need to buy a rubber chicken or do a tight three-minute comedy set to start your team meetings, but you might need to laugh more. Laughter is like air freshener that blows stale ideas and stagnant relationships out of the room. It lifts the fog of work and lets people catch their breath. It's especially powerful when it's unexpected—when people fear the worst and get something light-hearted instead.

One word of caution: If you use humor yourself, steer clear of sarcasm. It can lighten the mood momentarily, but it tends to do it at the expense of something or someone else. Some people have a knack for dry or dark humor, but most of us will find it unwieldy, so leave it to the pros. Instead, go for self-deprecating humor, the kind that points out your own foibles or limitations. It risks no one but yourself, and it demonstrates that everyone can and should laugh at themselves now and then.

2. Look for humor in the everyday

You don't necessarily need to be the source of humor yourself, but you need to model an appreciation for it. Life is full of humorous things. The question is whether you see them or not. (Incidentally, if you haven't encountered one recently, your work is getting the better of you, and you're missing some good stuff.) Sometimes, the best way to inject fun into your team is to simply make these things more visible.

When I was a university dean, I moved into an office with glass walls on two sides. It was located in the campus student center, so people regularly walked by and looked in at me. It was an uncomfortable arrangement. I felt like I was working inside an aquarium. On an odd impulse, I reflected this by posting a little sign on the outside of the glass that read:

The Dean of Students
Deanus Horribilus

Range: Campuswide
Habitat: Cafeterias, Classrooms, Residence Halls, and Racquetball Courts
Diet: Omnivorous. Special affinity for chocolate chip cookies and ice cream.

Figure 9.1

I realize this isn't a comedic masterpiece. It's just an acknowledgement of a peculiar situation, and it took less than five minutes to compose and post. But it became a source of humor and personal connection for the next several years.

People who looked into my office paused to read the sign and walked away smiling or pointing it out to their companions. On one lucky occasion, I received a burlap bag marked "Purina Dean Chow," and it was filled with chocolate chip cookies! Another time, I looked up from my desk to find a group of fifteen visitors outside the window. A campus tour guide was pointing at the sign and lecturing like a docent at a museum. Who knows what she was saying!

The point is, there's humor lurking in plain view, and all you need to do is point it out. You don't need to stage a major production or be a comedian yourself. It's often the "everydayness" of it that lightens the load, so the routine little things often mean more than the occasional big ones. It's quantity over quality, so the silly things, the corny things, the miscellaneous ironies and oddities that come up in conversation will suffice.

3. Take time to play

When there's lots of work to do, it's easy to feel like you can't afford to let anyone's attention stray from their tasks, but when it comes to kindling and keeping the fire in creatives, you can't afford *not* to. In fact, this is when play is most crucial, because people can't sustain constant exertion without diminished returns. Allowing or even incentivizing off-task behavior is most important when you need the on-task behavior to be productive, because the break refuels people physically and rejuvenates their imagination. Some organizations encourage such breaks by providing Ping-Pong, pool, or foosball tables and basketball hoops or dartboards. But special equipment isn't required. You can harness the refueling power of play with any diversion from work.

One team I work with is hooked on a game called Heads Up, a sort of app-assisted version of charades. They periodically drop what they are doing to play a few rounds, and after ten or fifteen minutes of silliness, they return to their work with renewed energy and focus.

My own team is currently waging war on another department in our building. Periodically, we press "pause" on what we're doing, grab our Nerf dart guns, and channel the stress of looming deadlines into bold frontal attacks on the enemy's territory. Typical skirmishes last only a few minutes, but they are full of shock and awe. Adrenaline surges in a withering barrage of Nerf products, rubber bands, and other aerodynamic office products. We laugh, do some high quality trash-talking, and then go back to the projects we left waiting on our desks.

Does this disrupt our work? Absolutely! But that's the point. We need the break and are reminding ourselves that our work is demanding but not all-consuming. We're mindful of the timing, and we respect when someone can't participate in the hostilities, but any time lost to the fun is more than recouped in our productivity and endurance over time.

If you want to fuel the fire in your team or refuel it when you see it burning low, you don't always need to turn up the heat. Sometimes you need to bring on the fun. Lighten up. Laugh a little. Add some humor and play some games. These things aren't as frivolous as you think. They are often your best investments in the innovation, collaboration, and stamina your team's been missing all along.

chapter ten

Trust:

Cultivating Psychological Safety for a Real Dream Team

If you want to go fast, go alone. If you want to go far, go together.

—African proverb

THERE'S NO DENYING the fact that the quality of outcomes is affected by the quality of the ingredients. The old programming adage of "garbage in: garbage out" is an apt warning to any of us looking to take shortcuts en route to an extraordinary goal. But it gets a little more complicated when it comes to assembling a great team of creatives. It's tempting to think that the secret to success is hiring top talent and assembling a creative dream team, but this is off base. Dream teams made up of individual superstars are notoriously disappointing.

The sports world is full of cautionary tales. For instance, in 2006, a U.S. baseball team stacked with all-stars like Roger Clemens, Derek Jeter, Alex Rodriguez, and Johnny Damon finished a disappointing fourth in the World Baseball Championships. These were some of the best-of-the-best competing in what is regularly referred to as "America's Pastime," yet they failed to impress. In the 2004 Olympics, the United States fielded a basketball team that was actually called the Dream Team in recognition of an impressive roster that included NBA standouts like LeBron James, Carmelo Anthony, Allen Iverson, Tim Duncan, Stephon Marbury, Dwayne Wade, and Amar'e Stoudemire; but it struggled throughout the games and barely bested Lithuania for a bronze medal. Again, the best ingredients failed to deliver the best results.

It appears that so-called dream teams are best crowned on the basis of their outcomes, not their composition. But if individual excellence is not a reliable path to top team performance, then what is? What fuels a great team?

Google has been fascinated by this same question and has tried to answer it by crunching massive amounts of data. In its Project Aristotle[6], it followed the activity of almost 200 of its own teams for a full year in hopes of identifying the perfect team composition, a sort of recipe for success. To their surprise, they discovered that the "who" of a team had little to do with its actual productivity. Teams with widely divergent participants performed very similarly, while teams with very similar participants and even overlapping membership performed differently. No reliable predictor of high performing teams emerged in terms of participants' personalities, skills, or backgrounds. So the researchers redirected their attention to the culture and norms of productive teams and discovered some interesting things. It turned out that the best teams at Google did have something in common. They weren't necessarily comprised of the best people, but each of them had a culture that enabled each member to consistently offer his or her best to the group. The climate in these teams was characterized by a high degree of what researchers call Psychological Safety.

Psychological Safety refers to the confidence you have that you can expose your real thoughts and feelings without the danger of being embarrassed, judged, or shut down by someone else. It's characterized by the kind of mutual respect and care that makes people willing to be themselves, and it's the core of what we often simply call trust.

Trust fuels the best collaborations and is a hallmark of the strongest teams. Where it exists, relationships are good. They are strong enough to flex and position themselves for the future. They are resilient enough to recover from missteps in the past or to bounce back from the dents and dings that scuff up every relationship over time. But where trust does not exist, relationships go bad. Even if they start out well, they spoil. People get prickly and fragile and keep lists of every slight. They develop complex rules of engagement, and relationships devolve into things that look like relationships but are really just practiced performances for specific audiences. Put simply, where there's trust, men and women are open, genuine, growing, and energized; but where there isn't, people are wary, inauthentic, self-preserving, and fatigued.

This means that when it comes to fueling the success of your creative team, the quality of what happens *between* members is more important than the quality of the members themselves. You don't need to fill your roster with superstars to accomplish great things as much as you need to collect talented people who play well together. Your best investments in firing up your team are the ones you make in developing psychological safety and trust among the creatives you lead. Unfortunately, this can be even trickier than simply shopping for superstars. It takes more than declaring your workspace a Psychological Safety Zone and more than a memo or a snappy new sign on the wall. Trust must be built, and it is built like anything substantial and enduring is ever built: step by step, a little at a time.

Some leaders fail to appreciate this and tell me, "I trust everyone until they give me a reason not to." I applaud the positive attitude they're trying to convey, but they're wrong. Trust doesn't work that way. It can't be assumed, because it is vulnerability-based and birthed only when you take interpersonal risks that are affirmed and supported. When you step out and make yourself vulnerable in small ways, the result you experience builds (or busts) the confidence you need to risk yourself in greater ways. As the people around you prove supportive, you feel psychologically safer, and your trust grows. Your willingness to be vulnerable increases, and you show them more and more of your true self. Conversely, if your trust is betrayed, you feel a greater need to protect yourself psychologically. Your willingness to expose yourself decreases, and you tend to be less vulnerable in the future. It's this process of testing that either leads toward trust or away from it, and it is not for the faint of heart. It takes a lot of courage to risk yourself this way, and sometimes that courage is hard to find. This is the reason trust is so important and also so rare.

If you want to encourage trust and foster the sense of psychological safety that will fuel your team and keep it fired up, then let me offer you three pieces of advice.

Be Careful with Competition

Despite their impressive talent, superstars aren't always inclined to help you in this endeavor. They may not contribute positively to psychological safety and may not be the best team players. Superstars are usually more accustomed to competing than collaborating. The route to superstardom runs through individual talent and achievement, so it's their ability to *separate* themselves from others that has distinguished them as, well... super. This disposition proves pretty useful in creating high caliber individual performers, but it's not so helpful in cultivating the kinds of players that contribute generously to a team. Most superstars have risen to the top of the pecking order by increasing the distance between themselves and everyone else, and they are prone to advance themselves, in part, by suppressing others. This principle is vividly illustrated by the genetic research of William Muir at Purdue University. In a study about the productivity of chickens (the original architects of the pecking order premise), he assembled a flock of what we might call superstar chickens. This was a Poultry Dream Team comprised of individual chickens that had distinguished themselves as especially good egg-layers. He also assembled a flock of what might be called Average Everyday Chickens, not especially impressive layers. He observed the two flocks and their egg production over time. After six generations, there were notable but surprising differences between the dream team and the everyday one.

The everyday flock was doing great. It's members were individually healthy, fully feathered, strong, and impressively productive. In fact, their egg laying had increased 160% since they were first assembled. By stark contrast, the supposed Dream Team was in disarray. After six generations of superstar-selective breeding, it had devolved into a battle dome of hyper-aggressive hens. Most of these standout chickens had been pecked to death by their peers, and only three bullied and unproductive hens still survived. Despite their individual prowess, the superstars didn't play nicely with others, and their overall productivity suffered.[7]

If you want your flock
of creatives to perform
well over time, then
you need to elevate
*collaboration over
competition.*

There's a lesson here for those who lead creatives. If you want your flock of creatives to perform well over time, then you need to elevate collaboration over competition. Make sure your model of success is an interdependent one that includes everyone. Obviously, the quality and quantity of individual contributions matter, but when you want to build trust, these factors are fostered best by focusing on the productivity of the team as a whole. Praise individuals that go out of their way to support others and to set goals that elevate collective rather than personal productivity. Above all, don't let individual performance eclipse or impair the team's.

One of the organizations I work with is unusually assertive about this principle. It's a tech company in the highly competitive healthcare industry, so it depends on top-notch talent; but it's leaders have decided it can't afford superstars who don't play well with others. They've codified this commitment in their motto: "No Brilliant Jerks." It's not just a cute saying, either. They're serious. They're convinced that their competitive advantage depends on their collaborative attitude, and they've demonstrated it by dismissing bona fide superstars who proved more concerned about their individual performance than the team's success.

If you want to increase the psychological safety that fuels creatives, be wary of competition. In small doses and friendly contexts, it might encourage performance, but typically only individual performance.

That's shortsighted or even counterproductive when it's collaboration that you really want. Instead, build a team of confidants and contributors who are interested in fanning the flames of each other's success.

Cultivate a Focus on Others

When your team members are attentive to each other, it's easier to keep their fire burning bright because they help fuel one another. Their focus on one another draws them closer together and enables them to be responsive and empathetic. Empathy is the ability to experience something from another person's point of view, to feel what he or she feels, even if it is notably different than what you would feel in the same situation. People who are self-centered have difficulty experiencing, let alone demonstrating, real empathy because they are stuck with only one vantage point on the world: their own. They often have trouble understanding others because they are simply more involved in trying to be understood themselves. When you encourage creatives to tune in to each other, you extend and broaden their perspectives. You enable them to relate to one another and to trust in deeper ways that get their fire going. In the best teams, members listen to one another patiently and demonstrate active listening skills like questioning, affirming, and reflecting. So, fuel your team by encouraging an others focus and modeling good listening skills and empathy.

As a bonus, you may find that encouraging creatives to focus on each other not only bolsters their psychological safety and builds trust, but also boosts their creativity over all. Research suggests that adopting an other-centered perspective can actually spur more creative thought and increase the number and quality of solutions generated. Professors Evan Polman and Kyle Emich, from NYU and Cornell University, respectively, demonstrated this by asking 137 undergraduates the following riddle:

"A prisoner was attempting to escape from a tower. He found a rope in his cell that was half as long enough to permit him to reach the ground safely. He divided the rope in half, tied the two parts together, and escaped. How could he have done this?"

(Pause for a moment and imagine yourself in the tower. How could you have accomplished this? I'll give you the solution in a moment...)

In the experiment, the professors asked half of the participants to imagine themselves as the prisoner locked in the tower. This is the same thing I asked you. They asked the other half of the participants to imagine *someone else* trapped in the tower. This is the same riddle but considered from a different vantage point. Could this simple difference in perspective affect the participants' ability to solve the riddle? The answer is yes.

In the first group, those with a subjective perspective, less than half (48%) of the participants actually came up with a solution, but in the second group, those with an other-centered perspective, nearly two-thirds (66%) got it right. They figured out that the prisoner split the rope lengthwise and tied the pieces together to double the total length.[8]

This, and the results of similar experiments, suggests that when we think of our own situations, we tend to think more concretely and find it more difficult to suspend reality and generate new ideas. But when we think about others' situations, we tend to think broadly and more abstractly, and it's easier to generate creative options. So, the next time you need more creative answers, ask your team to adopt an other-centered perspective. Don't ask them what they would do in the situation; ask them what someone else would do. It's a subtle difference that pays off because it's easier to think outside the box if you don't envision yourself in the box to begin with.

Create Interdependence

Putting competition in its place and cultivating an other-centered perspective fosters the trust that fuels great teams, but requiring team members to depend upon each other deepens it over time. Interdependence is like the gym, where trust works out and grows strong. It's the crux of what it takes to build strong teams.

When leaders call me to do some "teambuilding," they are almost always looking for a way to increase the trust among their team members. They hope that an afternoon of discussion and group exercises with me will transform the dynamics in their team and leave members feeling psychologically safer and more inclined to work with each other. I try to let them down easy. There are some things I can do to illuminate issues and start them down the road to building trust, but there's not a lot I can do to change the hearts and minds of participants in a few hours. If they are looking for a quick way to make a big difference, they should forget the dispositions of their team and reconsider the structure of the game they are playing together.

The structure of work either leads people toward trust, by requiring them to depend on one another, or away from it, by allowing them to be independently successful. Trust is built through interdependence. It's forged in the risks of relying on each other, and people aren't typically inclined to take such risks if they don't have to. So, if the path to success does not require interdependence, then people will go it alone, and trust won't develop in the team. Put more simply, if people can be successful individually, they won't depend on others, and trust won't grow.

If you want to foster teamwork and build trust among creatives, it's often better to change the processes than the perspectives. Instead of convening warm, fuzzy encounter sessions where you praise the power of teamwork, restructure the process of the work itself so that success requires interdependence. When creatives must rely on each other to advance, they get real and put trust on the table. Their individual desires to succeed will draw them into the kinds of interactions that create and strengthen psychological safety and fuel the fire in their team.

The author C. S. Lewis provides a beautiful picture of trust and teamwork that summarizes the ideas in this chapter. It illustrates how a team can be fueled and can achieve success when it stops competing and starts focusing and depending on one another. In his book, *The Great Divorce*, he describes two versions of eternity. Each features a banquet table filled with delicious food and surrounded by hungry guests who have 3-foot-long utensils attached to their hands. At one table, the guests struggle futilely to feed themselves. The length of the utensils foils every attempt, and they can't get the delicious food into their mouths. Consequently, they are famished and grow increasingly angry. Their gathering is filled with frustration and discord. This is Lewis' depiction of Hell.

At the other table, the circumstances are the same, but the atmosphere is very different. Here the guests appear well-fed and satisfied. Laughter and friendly conversation fill the room. This is his depiction of Heaven. At this banquet, each guest is using the 3-foot-long utensil to feed the person across the table.

If you want to fuel the fire in your creatives and lead a dream team of your own, here's a good recipe. Start with the right ingredients: talented people who want to both dream *and* contribute to a team. Combine with a liberal helping of challenges and opportunities, and mix well. Go easy on the competition. Add a focus on others and some genuine interdependence, and let it cook. Serves everyone.

chapter eleven

Purpose:

Pumping Up Purpose to Battle Burnout & Build Buy-In

There are two great days in a person's life—the day we are born and the day we discover why.

—William Barclay

THREE QUESTIONS CIRCULATE at the center of interactions between leaders and their teams: Why? What? and How? Of the three, Why is the shyest. What and How are noisy by nature, boisterously asserting themselves in the midst of other conversations. They're prominent on to-do lists and timecards, and they turn up regularly in conversations about productivity. Why, however, is a wallflower. It is always waiting for someone to invite it in and make space for it in the hubbub. It is disturbingly content to take a back seat in the busyness, and it often gets left out of the conversation altogether as What and How rattle on.

When you lead creatives, you can't let this happen. What and How may be the wheels of an organization's progress, but Why is the fuel on which its people run. If the What and How drown out the Why, people will find themselves busy but purposeless, and that's a bad combination. People in general and creatives in particular are creatures of conviction. They run on a sense of purpose, and when they lack it, they break down. They run out of fuel, and the fire that inspires and animates them goes out.

Viktor E. Frankl, the Austrian psychiatrist, observed this during his internment in a Nazi concentration camp during World War II. In that horrible and hopeless place, he discovered that having a purpose could transform the experience of suffering and make the difference between whether a person lived or died. He wrote the following in his book, *Man's Search for Meaning*, originally published in German in 1946:

> A man who becomes conscious of the responsibility he bears toward a human being who affectionately waits for him, or to an unfinished work, will never be able to throw away his life. He knows the "why" for his existence, and will be able to bear almost any "how."[9]

A connection with a greater purpose reframed prisoners' immediate circumstances and enabled them to transcend them. Prisoners who became disconnected from the Why lost hope, became discouraged, and were consumed.

In the less dire world of your own work, you can see the same principle playing out. When creatives and their colleagues have a clear sense of purpose, they are fully fueled, resilient, and capable of extraordinary contributions and accomplishments. The Why draws them forward when the What and How are daunting or uninspiring, and they are willing to give generously to the endeavor and to each other. But when they lack a sense of purpose, it's a different story. They are different people, fearful, self-protecting, miserly with their investments, fragile, and prone to derailment and disillusionment by little things.

To keep creatives fired up and kindle the fire that warms them to the task and to each other, you need to keep the purpose preeminent. When they know the Why, they are more likely to commit and endure. So fueling their sense of purpose is like stoking the fire in their bellies. It's the secret to building buy-in and battling burnout in your team.

Building Buy-In

I was recently flipping channels and marveling at the barrage of infomercials on late-night TV. I learned about stain removal, slicing things, and the wonders of nonstick cooking. I also learned that the men and women pitching these products are amazingly persuasive. I found myself thinking, "You know, he's right... I probably *do* need a special gizmo to pull weeds the *correct* way," and, "She's got a point... I *would* be a lot happier if my kitchen knives could saw a brick in half."

The products they were pushing were intriguing, but it wasn't the product that drew me in, it was the *deal*. It was the idea that I could have such life-changing gizmos at such low, low prices. (In fact, I could have a second set of the steak knives for free if I called right away!)

In my experience, many leaders think of themselves as pitchmen or pitchwomen, too. Like salespeople, they describe the future in ways that inspire action, and their roles require them to sell their teams on ideas or courses of action. Even their motivational vocabulary is filled with sales jargon. They *sell* people on a vision, cultivate *buy-in* from stakeholders, and talk about ROI (returns on investment) in development plans and performance reviews. But leaders are not pitchmen and pitchwomen in at least one important respect: They are not simply wooing people toward a new idea or opportunity; they are trying to create genuine commitment to it over time.

I suspect that the late night hucksters I was watching cared more about eliciting my immediate response than cultivating my commitment. They wanted me to grab my credit card and call now because quantities were limited and operators were standing by. By contrast, leaders need to inspire more than impulsive action. They need to build real buy-in and cause their teams to step up to greater and greater accountability in the service of their commitments. This takes more than the prospect of a great deal. It takes a compelling purpose, and, more importantly, it takes a leader with the courage to tell the potentially unappealing truth about what serving that purpose will cost.

Many leaders miss this. Like infomercial spokespeople, they try to enlist others in their endeavors by pitching the best deals they can describe. When they need people to step up or redirect their activity, these leaders try to make the changes sound as minimal and manageable as possible. "There won't be too many extra hours required." "The project won't last all that long." "There will be new synergies and shortcuts that offset any increased demands." "The change isn't really *that* big, and the transition won't take *that* long." They are convinced that people will move in new directions or buy in to new ideas best if the cost appears inconsequential.

There's just enough truth in this to convince you that it is the secret to motivating behavior and leading change. Unfortunately, you'll discover this technique is *only* about behavior, and it secretly drains the buy-in of your creatives even as it temporarily elevates or redirects their activity.

Here's why: It isn't crazy to think that people respond to a good deal, but that's focusing on the wrong side of the equation. When you do that, you're trying to sweeten the deal by making the investment seem less consequential, instead of by making the return seem more worthy. As a result, your team will be willing to do what you ask but with no increased commitment to the goals you want to achieve. The interaction won't move them forward in capacity and commitment as much as it will simply convince them that what you're asking isn't troubling enough to resist. This might get things moving, but it also makes the deal fragile and prone to failure as soon as things get uncomfortable or demanding. And, let's face it, every important endeavor eventually gets uncomfortable and demanding.

If you don't want your team to bail when the going gets tough, then you need to elevate their commitment as well as their activity. You need them to believe in what they're doing enough to *want* to give generously of their time and talent. This means that you need to talk more about the purpose than the investments if you want them to have enough fuel for the exertion of following through. You need to be more preacher than pitchman. When people are struggling under the weight of the What and How, they don't always need you to lighten their load. They need you to make them stronger to carry it; they need to know the Why. When you want to build buy-in, pump up the purpose. Never lowball the investment. Instead, tell 'em why it's worth all they've got.

When they are fully fueled with purpose, they are also more likely to be proud of their investments over time. Buyer's remorse may be a small concern for the infomercial pitchman, but it's a big one for you because you're looking for more than a one-time response. You need a team that comes back for more and regularly reinvests. That means that you don't simply want compliance; you want commitment. Of course, you need both compliance and commitment to succeed, but they are not the same thing, and you need to be savvy about which one you seek and when.

Compliance is about getting the right action, moving people's hands and feet. Commitment is about getting the right convictions, moving people's hearts. Compliance might look good at the moment, but it's a pale substitute for real commitment because it isn't fueled by purpose and easily disappears under fire. You need to be wary of being satisfied with behavior when what you really want is buy-in. Commitment never exists without action, but action frequently exists without commitment. Fueling your team with purpose requires you to look past the activity of your team and decide if their Why is lacking. If it is, pump up the purpose again.

Battling Burnout

Pumping up the purpose also prepares your team to endure. It gives creatives fuel to burn when the heat is on. Once they've bought into your mission, you need them to persist until it's accomplished, and people who lack purpose don't last very long. A strong work ethic might sustain them for a time, but purposeless people eventually feel unfulfilled and overworked. They burn out and leave, or worse, they burn out and stay!

Leaders often think of burnout as a workload problem, but that perspective only considers the What and How and misses the deeper issue. Burnout is mostly about the Why. It may be accelerated by overwork, but it is fundamentally the result of an emotional, spiritual, or existential deficit. People don't burn out from too much to do, but from too little reason to do it. That's why people with relatively light loads can burn out, too. If you want to prevent burnout and keep creatives burning bright, you should worry less about whether they are overworked than whether they are under-purposed.

Worn Out *Need rest, recovery*	Burnt Out *Need purpose*
Fatigued/Physically Tired	Emotionally/Spiritually Spent/ Empty/Depleted
Useful/Hopeful/Meaningful	Useless/Hopeless/Meaningless
Bounces Back	No Resilience
Episodic/Temporary	Unrelenting/Persistent

Figure 11.1

When people work hard, they get tired; but physical fatigue isn't always a bad thing. It indicates you're reaching the limits of your physical strength, but it is temporary and recoverable. Sometimes fatigue is the hallmark of a meaningful contribution or great work, a badge of honor for a big thing done well. For example, I enjoy yard work. It's where I exercise and exorcise all kinds

People don't burn out from too much to do, but from *too little reason to do.*

Dr. Andrew Johnston | 151

of stresses in my life, so my idea of a great Saturday is to work in the yard from sunup to sundown. At the end of the day, I am exhausted, but it's that "good tired" that accompanies satisfying work. I'm worn out, but not burnt out. I'll take a shower, sleep well, and be eager to do it again the next week.

Similarly, periodic fatigue in your team shouldn't trouble you. It's part of the bargain when you are accomplishing big things. It's the feeling that signals that a huge project is finally delivered or a major performance has taken place. It's the natural consequence of creatives making extravagant contributions to a meaningful purpose. It's the sign that they've given it everything they've got. Celebrate it and give them time to recover, and they'll be eager to do it again.

Burnout, however, is a different story. It isn't that "good tired" that strengthens you spiritually even as it fatigues you physically. It's the "bad tired" that depletes you altogether. A nap isn't going to power you up when it's purpose that you're lacking. Reducing the workload isn't going to make much of a difference, either. In fact, taking the wrong responsibilities off the list can make the experience feel even more pointless and exacerbate the problem. You might delay the inevitable by lightening the load, but to successfully battle burnout, you need to pump up the purpose.

You need to make more room for the Why. When the Why is strong, people can handle a lot more of the What and How. They're fully fueled, so they don't run

___

When the *Why* is
strong, people can
handle a lot more of the
What and *How*.

out of gas as quickly when life gets consuming. Spend time discussing the purpose behind the projects, and don't be afraid to push the reasons for them as high as possible. The loftier the purpose, the more the difficulty and effort to achieve it become incidental because creatives have fuel to burn. What and How will always get their due, because you can't delegate tasks or contribute to a project without engaging them. However, your focus should be on levering the Why into as many conversations as possible.

I find that leaders often *think* about the Why because they tend to be strategic minded, but they still fail to *say* anything about it. Maybe they figure everyone else is thinking about it, too. Maybe they just take it for granted, or, worse, they don't believe purpose is pertinent at the lower levels of an organization. Whatever the reason, it's a mistake, and they're missing the best opportunity to inoculate their people against burnout. Don't let the purpose get left out or float around separated from the daily doing in your team. Link the two and articulate the connection every chance you get.

Overall, purpose proves to be some of the most potent fuel you can offer your team because it doesn't just fire them up, it keeps them burning over time. It fills them up and motivates them intrinsically. Extrinsic motivators, like promises and threats, or carrots and sticks, can kick up the fire in a team, too, but in a very different way. The fire they kindle is a flash fire. It burns bright and hot, but it quickly consumes the fuel and goes out again. Leaders who rely on these tactics find it difficult to keep their people fired up. They are perpetually turning up the heat or fanning the dying flames to no avail. They're always struggling with buy-in and burnout in their teams. There is no way around it. When the fuel is gone, the fire is, too. So, if you want to kindle the kind of fire that keeps burning, fuel your creatives with an abundance of purpose. Pile on the Why and light it up.

HEAT

You can't get ignition without sufficient heat because of something called the "kindling point." This is the point at which a substance will combust, and if you can't get the temperature above it, you'll see only smoke, not fire. Similarly, if you're a leader who doesn't want to turn up the heat on the people and projects you lead, you may find yourself longing for ignition in your team. You may be poised for great things but never achieve them, because it's too easy for your team to avoid the investments that accompany high standards and hard work.

Like it or not, leadership isn't simply about inspiring people with lofty goals. It's about motivating people to reach them. It's not just about firing people up; it's about lighting a fire underneath them. Great leaders push, pull, and preach their teams toward high aspirations. They can be drill sergeants as well as cheerleaders and can deliver a kick in the pants as well as a pat on the back.

It's the heat that turns great potential into reality—a bonfire is just a pile of sticks without it. Similarly, you can assemble all the talents in the world and give them room to breathe, but if you are unable or unwilling to light a fire under them, you won't see what they can really do.

The chapters in this section prepare you to turn up the heat by setting ambitious goals, clarifying expectations, giving feedback, and embracing the risks that accompany extraordinary things.

chapter twelve

Challenge:

Triggering Flow by Turning Up the Challenge

The best moments in our lives are not the passive, receptive, relaxing times... The best moments usually occur if a person's body or mind is stretched to its limits in a voluntary effort to accomplish something difficult and worthwhile.

—Mihaly Csikszentmihalyi

WHEN THE HEAT is on, people get focused and fired up. Have you ever been in a challenging situation where you are totally consumed by what you're doing? My son describes it when he's rock climbing. He gets so focused on the problem at hand or the next move he's going to make that the rope, the height, and the rest of the world just disappear. He's completely absorbed, fully focused, and fired up.

Maybe you've felt this way, too, in a project, a sport, or a performance of some kind. Your full attention was directed at your movements and what you were going to do next. You were able to see the situation perfectly, and there was no confusion or conflict because you couldn't afford those things. There was too much at stake, but you weren't anxious or stressed out. In fact, you felt terrific, fearless. Your actions felt almost effortless. If

3 33 3 3 3 3 3 3 3 3 3 3 3 3 3 3 3 3 3 3 3 3

you've felt this way, you've experienced a peculiar and potent mental state known as Flow.

Hungarian psychologist Mihaly Csikszentmihalyi originally coined the term Flow in the 1980s to represent a mental state linked with "optimal performance." He described it as an experience where the mental, creative, and physical boundaries that typically constrain people seem to disappear, leaving them more capable, more resilient, and happier as a result[10]

Flow is an immersive, consuming experience where a person is concentrating so hard that he doesn't even realize he is doing it, and anything other than the object of that concentration disappears. Time dilates or expands or simply becomes irrelevant, and physical needs like hunger, pain, and fatigue fade into the background. Flow creates a special space, in the midst of everything else, that is free of distractions and full of opportunity. That's why athletes often refer to it as simply being "in the zone."

Flow has special implications for creatives, because it has a unique way of firing them up and setting their imaginations free. During Flow, brain activity changes, and brainwaves move in a sort of imaginative sweet spot. In our normal waking interactions, our brains function in fast-moving beta waves; but in Flow, everything slows down, and there are more alpha waves and theta waves. Alpha waves are typically associated with daydreaming, and theta waves usually signal the REM state we float through when we are falling sleep. In other words, the Flow state literally changes our minds and produces a kind of "dreamy" territory where our thoughts are more fluid and ideas are birthed more easily. In this zone, creatives can move among their ideas quickly and manipulate or connect them in new ways more easily.

Flow also frees creatives from the self-doubt and inner criticism that can dampen their creative thinking. During Flow, a part of the brain called the prefrontal cortex powers down. This is the part of the brain that maintains our sense of self, and this adjustment is why we lose ourselves in our experience when we are in the zone. It's also the part of our brain where our "inner critic" lives, that nagging voice that edits us and keeps our imaginations close to home. So, when this part is largely offline, the critic's voice is silenced. Our self-monitoring and impulse controls are diminished, and this makes us less likely to second-guess ourselves. We are less encumbered by fear or other boundaries.

All of this means that Flow enables creatives to be more imaginatively bold, to envision and enact extraordinary things, and to be more resilient and fulfilled while they are doing it. That makes Flow an especially "flammable" condition you will want to cultivate if in order to kindle and keep the fire burning in your team. To foster it, pay attention to the level of challenge your creatives face and be prepared to turn up the heat.

People only enter the flow state when the pressure is on and performance matters, so you make it more likely when you keep things challenging. Csikszentmihalyi illustrates this in his "Map of everyday Experience."

Map of Everyday Experience

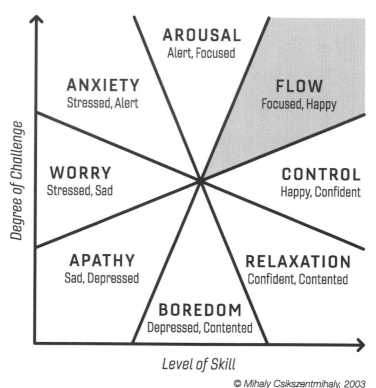

© Mihaly Csikszentmihaly, 2003

Figure 12.1

This diagram describes how people's emotional postures change based on the relationship between their competence and the challenges they face. Think of it as a temperature gauge. In general, it clarifies that people feel the heat when the challenge exceeds their skill, but they are pretty chill when their skill exceeds the challenge. If you want to trigger Flow in your team, then you need to manage the challenge well. When the level of challenge is too low, it won't merit creatives' utmost attention, and they will go through the motions but not be consumed in the way that initiates Flow. They will disengage cognitively and be active but not activated. On the other hand, if the level of challenge is too daunting, it won't fire them up, either. It will cause them to disengage emotionally or physically, and they will fail to enter Flow. Only when the challenge is pitched right will creatives find it worthy of their full talent and attention and will experience the magical intersection of action and awareness we call Flow. This often means that the best thing you can do for your team is to turn up the heat.

Turn Up the Heat, Turn On the Flow

I learned this myself when I faced a leadership challenge several years ago. I was the Dean of Students at Belmont University, and I was leading a team of talented professionals into a season where both the quality and quantity of their work would need to increase. Our division's successes in the previous year had created new opportunities that would increase the expectations and workload for my team as we moved forward. I would need to ask my people to step up and do more and I was dreading it because I knew they felt like they'd already reached the limits of their capacity. Frankly, I thought they had, too, but I had no choice. I couldn't add more people, so I needed the current ones to find another gear, some way to make bigger and better contributions. I needed them to find their Flow.

If Flow is characterized by the confluence of high competency and high challenge, and my people were already highly competent, then I realized that I might need to turn up the challenge to get them "in the zone." This was not an appealing option, because my team was already working very hard. They were feeling major pressure to perform, and the idea of increasing the challenge seemed foolhardy and frustrating, but the more I reflected on Csikszentmihalyi's ideas, the more it rang true.

I began to recognize that my team was busy but not necessarily fulfilled. I had highly skilled people, but their experience was characterized more by perspiration than inspiration, and that's a recipe for burnout, not Flow. I began to wonder if they had been laboring in a sort of stressful pre-Flow state where the goals were heavy but "ho-hum," requiring significant investment from people but not feeling worth it in the end. I came to the conclusion that if I wanted them to experience the wonders of Flow, I had to actually *increase* the challenge they faced. Here are some tactics that helped me turn up the heat without turning off the team.

———

Leaders looking for
Flow need to dial up
the worth, not the work.

Set Scary Goals

Increasing the level of challenge isn't simply about making people busier. In fact, busywork is a Flow-inhibiter. When people have an abundance of tasks that take their time without meriting their talent, they quickly wear out and underperform mentally and physically. Leaders looking for Flow need to dial up the worth, not the work. They need to make sure that skilled people have the opportunity to expend their talents on truly worthy goals.

With this in mind, I determined to set goals for my team that were more compelling. I described this in principle to supervisors as we entered our annual planning process. I told them I was looking for aspirations that were lofty enough to matter and to prompt real emotional responses in the people pursuing them. When I received the proposed goals, I was disappointed. They were significant, but they didn't sing. I feared they still lurked in that dangerous heavy-but-ho-hum territory that wouldn't trigger Flow. So I sent them back to the supervisors and asked for revisions. Specifically, I asked them to make the goals "scary". I know this is an odd descriptor to use, maybe even negative or off-putting to some, but I found it struck the right chord in practice. I wanted them to describe targets that frightened them a little because they were important but not certain to be accomplished. I was looking for something right at the edge of their ability to achieve.

When they came back with these revised, "scarier" goals, I asked if they thought they could achieve them, and I listened very carefully to their responses. In my experience, people often set goals they are confident they can achieve. They want to win, and sometimes they improve their chances by naming easier targets. It's like a coach managing his record by playing only teams he knows he can win. This is no way to foster Flow, because it produces a laudable record of performance with a lagging sense of personal achievement. When I listened to responses, I listened for commitment more than confidence. I wanted to hear that supervisors thought a goal was genuinely *worthy* of their investment even if they worried about their ability to achieve it. If supervisors sounded too sure of achieving the goal, like it was a foregone conclusion, I asked them to make it "scarier".

Over time, I found that you could tell when a goal presented a promising degree of challenge by the way it sounded and the way people talked about it. Goals that were pitched too low didn't evoke any real emotional response. As a result, the goal itself came up less in conversation than the uninspiring details of what people had to do to serve it. By contrast, a goal that was pitched high enough really preached. It caught your attention or impressed you a little when someone said it. It inspired people, and they referenced it with pride. It gave meaning to the efforts they put into it, so they naturally reminded one other of what they were trying to achieve.

In the end, a call for Scary Goals produced targets that were challenging in the right ways and big enough and meaningful enough to get people in the Flow zone.

Match People with the Challenge

Flow is not a collective experience; it's an individual one. When athletes and others are in the zone, they may appear to collaborate with others or contribute to a team's success, but their actual experience is separate from all of that. The hyper-focus that accompanies Flow keeps these external things at a distance, and they are fully absorbed in their own individual activity. For this reason, if you want to foster Flow in your team, you need to foster it individually. Metaphorically, you need to play chess, not checkers.

Chess and Checkers have some similarities in form and strategy, but they differ greatly in one way: the pieces themselves. In checkers, the pieces are identical. You can win by employing them interchangeably in your strategy. In chess, the pieces are different and move in particular ways, so you can only win by employing them correctly. A winning strategy employs the right piece at the right time for the right purpose.

This is the same mindset that enables you to calibrate challenge and foster Flow in your team. Your team members are not identical or interchangeable; they are individuals. Their talents are different, and their skill levels vary. So tuning the level of challenge to produce

Flow must be individualized, too. One size does not fit all. You need to assign the right tasks to the right people so that the level of challenge pushes but does not exceed their competence. In my experience, most leaders don't know the things they need to know to make such individualized decisions. Their awareness of the projects and players is too broad, too globalized, so they wind up playing checkers in spite of their intentions. If you want to foster Flow, then you need to know enough about your people and the potential assignments to match them well. It's worth your time and effort because there's a lot riding on it. When you get the match right, you stretch creatives in ways that reinforce intrinsic motivation and trigger Flow. If you get it wrong, you insulate them from that state and leave them bored or overwhelmed. Look closely at your team members to understand their individual talents and skills and become a master match-maker. Think carefully about how assignments will stretch or challenge individuals and make the connections that foster Flow.

Keep the focus on the goal

Flow is hyper-focused. It blurs and distances noise, distractions, and anything other than the immediate task. It's this clarity that makes the engagement so pure, uncomplicated, and intrinsically motivating. It enables people to transcend the things that usually limit them.

Csikszentmihalyi puts it this way in *Flow: The Psychology of Optimal Experience*, "...It is when we act freely, for the sake of the action itself rather than for ulterior motives, that we learn to become more than what we were."[10] This connection to intrinsic motivation makes Flow especially suited to creatives, but it also makes it tricky to foster when there are so many competing motivations at hand.

To foster Flow, you must keep creatives focused on the worthy goals you've identified and help them resist other common motivators that might distract them. Here are a few motivators to be wary of. They might spur activity toward a goal, but they will never foster Flow.

THE REQUIREMENT TO DO IT. Flow is fostered when people voluntarily commit their energy and talents to worthy tasks. This means that it is triggered only by their own volition. When you motivate people by reminding them that they have no choice, you are likely to get activity, but it's not the kind of unusual performance and attention that comes with Flow.

THE RELIEF OF BEING DONE. When people are working hard, it's tempting to encourage them by reminding them how good it will feel to be done. This may motivate them for a time, but for the wrong reasons. They're moved more to stop than to finish, and they are no longer focusing on the worthiness of the goal as much as the appeal of no longer serving it. Flow can't happen if people are thinking beyond the experience at hand.

THE COMPENSATION FOR DOING IT. Incentives are powerful things, but they are dangerous when it comes to fostering Flow. Cash, prizes, rewards, and consequences motivate people extrinsically and divert attention from the actual goal to the carrot or even the stick being used to dangle it. As a result, they always dilute the inherent value of the experience itself. To foster Flow, compensate people fairly, but then turn their attention away from payroll and perks toward the worthiness of the task itself.

Don't Pull the Bar Down

As I conclude this chapter, I want to illuminate a Flow-busting temptation that arises for every leader at some point, especially when they are feeling the heat themselves. That is the temptation to change the goal and lower expectations when the going gets tough. Every leader feels the tug of this temptation now and then. If you're empathetic and tuned in to your team, then you may feel it all the time. It comes when you've done all the right things to foster Flow. You've set scary goals, matched people with them well, and kept the focus where it belongs; but now things are getting tough. People are paying the price for the height of the aspirations, and you are tempted to lower the bar to ease their pain. Don't do it!

If the level of challenge is right, it pushes people to their limits. This is uncomfortable, but it is also the threshold of Flow. It's the peculiar stress and opportunity of this position that triggers the release of the neurochemicals that increase attention, speed up heart rate and respiration, ease pain, and inhibit fear. Pulling the bar down at this point leaves people stuck in the worst spot of all: maximum effort with minimal benefit and reward. It's a total Flow-buster.

Think of it this way: At this point, your team has given so much to the project that lowering the goal won't alleviate any negative impacts of that investment, but it will diminish the satisfaction they'll feel when they're done. You have good intentions, but your tactic is going to impact the worth more than the work. In this situation, the best thing you can do to foster Flow and honor your creatives is to safeguard the trophy that is waiting for them when they finish. Keep the heat on and have courage. If you've set the bar right to begin with, then you will serve your team best by keeping it high when it's hard.

chapter thirteen

Expectations:

Clarifying Success & Failure

We run to win, not just to be in the race.

—Vince Lombardi

YOUR TEAM'S SUCCESS often depends upon on your ability to keep it moving in the right direction. You need to keep the heat on the right things, and keep the most important things from being put on the back burner. In this endeavor, the classic To-Do list proved to be one of the sneakiest success killers around. I know this sounds odd to say because there is genuinely so much to do in today's busy workplaces, and so many voices, podcasts, apps, and infomercials are devoted to keeping track of it all. But the typical To-Do list doesn't direct your creatives toward success, because it's designed to keep track of activity, not progress. Activity is all about motion in the moment. It's satisfied when you look around the room and see that each member of your team is busy. Progress, however, is all about movement toward the goal; and it's only satisfied when the distance between you and your aspiration disappears.

The typical To-Do list is a poor tool for illuminating this distance, because it focuses attention on the tasks that are instrumental to achieving a goal instead of on the goal itself. As a result, people become less clear about what they are producing than about how busy they should be with the producing of it. This puts the heat on the wrong things and encourages creatives to burn for minor tasks instead of lofty aspirations. When this happens, activity might increase, but progress is hard to find. It's like telling a construction crew all about the hammering and the sawing you need without giving them blueprints or pictures of the house you want to build. Determining progress and directing the work gets difficult when the crew thinks more about whether they are hammering and sawing enough than about whether or not the house is coming together as intended.

I suppose leaders need to worry about keeping people busy, too, but the teams I serve are rarely struggling with the fact that they aren't *doing* enough. They are struggling with the fact that they aren't *accomplishing* enough, and that's a problem To-Do lists can't solve.

The key to clarifying progress and keeping your team focused on success is to look past the tasks and make sure they know exactly what success looks like. Think of the endeavor as a race your team wants to win. Your job is to establish a vivid finish line and cheer them on. They're eager to break the tape, not just run fast; but if you don't tell them exactly where they're headed, they're likely to get lost along the way.

I decided to test this principle by pranking some preschool children. Well, in retrospect, I confess it looks like a prank; but at the time, I thought of it as a serious sociological experiment. The subjects, er... kids, were outside playing on the playground when I called them over and asked if they would like to participate in a race. It took only a little enthusiasm and psyching up from me to produce five highly motivated little racers who were fired up and raring to go. I laid a stick on the ground and told them it was the starting line. They crowded behind it and started jockeying for position. I asked them if they were ready to go, and they nodded. "Are you suuuuuure you're ready?" I asked, and they nodded even more enthusiastically. "You're positive that you're ready to run really, *reeeaaally* fast?" I asked, and they shouted back, "Yes!" So I yelled, "Go!"

Now, as you are reading this, you may notice that I've left out one ingredient of a typical race: the finish line. It isn't just something I failed to note in my description to you; it's something I never mentioned to the racers, either. I clarified the starting line, I psyched them up, and I repeatedly emphasized the need to run fast. But I never identified or even referenced a finish line. Surprisingly, this didn't seem to faze them at all. They enthusiastically lined up at the start and leaped into action the moment I shouted "Go," but what they did next tells us a lot about what it's like to chase an illusive or ill-defined goal.

When I shouted, "Go!" four children left the line. (The fifth child simply started running in place enthusiastically.) Of the four kids that came out of the blocks strong, two ran hard for about five or six yards and stopped, looking a bit confused. They turned around, and one of them said, "Where's the end?" A third racer, upon hearing this, slowed down and stopped a little farther away. The final racer never even paused or looked back. He ran straight ahead for about 30 yards and then kept running at full speed in a broad circle encompassing the entire playground! By the time I opened my mouth to respond to the initial question, two of those who had stopped had started chasing each other and were now weaving off among other kids on the playground, their race apparently forgotten.

The images of these would-be racers still flash through my mind when I'm working with organizations that have unclear or ill-conceived goals. In these situations, the leaders are a lot like me on the playground. They aren't so much directing their people as much as they are simply revving them up and telling them to run fast. Consequently, the results they get don't look so different from the ones in my "experiment." Some of their people run in place. They don't know where they're going, but they're good workers and will content themselves with simply being busy. Some of their people enjoy the thrill of motion, so they create their own goals and run off in directions that suit them but may or may not be in the best interest of the organization.

Most of their people get lost somewhere in the tension of trying to run well with no way to get their bearings or gauge their progress. They run and then stop, try to run again, lose their direction or their confidence, and eventually start picking at each other or wandering off, wondering why they got involved in the first place.

These things can happen in any collaborative endeavor, as it's easy for activity to replace progress in the minds of busy people. The danger of this is especially present in creative endeavors, because the creative process itself is so consuming and rewarding. When they are immersed in the experience, creatives can quickly lose sight of what it's for or where it's going and wander off. They need their leader to do more than simply psych them up and say, "Run fast!" They need you to give them a clear finish line. To keep the charms and challenges of the work itself from eclipsing what it is supposed to accomplish, you need to describe success and clarify failure in no uncertain terms.

Describe Success Clearly and Concretely

As a fellow leader, I'm surprised and embarrassed at how often I simply assume that my team knows what we're trying to accomplish. We make lists and have meetings about the things we need to do. We sweat the deadlines and work hard, but if you asked my team members what success looks like, I'm not sure you'd get the same answer from each of them. I'm pretty confident you'd get *good* answers from them, but that's not the same thing. If I want them to work most effectively as a team and coordinate their efforts best, then I need them all to be running the exact same race. You do, too, and that means that each of your team members, like mine, needs to have the same finish line in sight. To that end, you need to describe what success looks like in no uncertain terms.

In my experience, you should be able to do this in one or two sentences. If it takes more than that, be wary. You may not be communicating as precisely as you need to be, and the goal may not be as clear to your people as you think it is. They may get the gist of it, but they may still be running in several different directions at once. You want to minimize interpretations and different perspectives on success so that the finish line is not obscured by the cloud of competing agendas and negotiations that often arise when people run fast.

To this end, if it were up to me, I would outlaw the use of the word "excellence." I'd cut it out of the leadership lexicon and make everyone operationalize what he or she means by it instead. I'm convinced that we'd all be better off. I'll admit, excellence is a good thing; we all agree on that. It's touted by everyone from teachers and top executives to advertisers and athletic coaches. But it's also a completely abstract and unspecific thing, so it inspires people's aspirations without informing their practice. When leaders use it to describe success, their teams know they are supposed to do something great, but they're not exactly sure what it is. It's a lot like shouting, "Run fast!"

It's also hard to describe success clearly and succinctly for your team if the goal is not as clear to you as it needs to be. Leaders spend a lot of time thinking about success, but that doesn't necessarily make things any clearer. When a person spends a lot of time thinking about something, it's easy to mistake familiarity for clarity.

You might recognize this distinction from your school days if you ever anticipated a multiple-choice test and it turned out to be essay or short answer. You were prepared to recognize the right answer, but you couldn't come up with it on your own. That's familiarity, not clarity.

If you are a busy leader, you can be immersed in so many strategic considerations that you employ a sort of mental shorthand to manage them all. This makes the barrage more manageable in your mind, but it doesn't necessarily make the goals clearer or prepare you for communicating clear finish lines to your team. You need to get more specific and concrete.

For this reason, I encourage you to determine what success looks like and write it down. Your own ideas get clearer when you try to articulate them, because the discipline of crafting the right language reveals assumptions and drives out abstraction. The act of writing will distill your thoughts, discipline your communication, and prepare you to paint a finish line for your team in unmistakable terms. It also creates something that can be specifically revisited or revised, as necessary, down the road.

Leaders of creatives sometimes balk at this suggestion, because they fear it will constrain the imagination of their teams. They are concerned that defining success too concretely will prevent creatives from thinking outside the box. But being concrete is not the same thing as being narrow. It's about describing the destination unmistakably, not about telling people how to run (or the route they must take, for that matter). Most professional creative endeavors are undertaken in the service of something else—conveying a point or provoking a response, adding meaning or fostering an emotion, etc. These are the things that need to be clearly identified so that creatives can effectively direct and test their efforts to achieve them. In practice, imagination soars in the service of concrete goals because when everyone has the same idea of success, they can be even more creative and collaborative in pursuing it.

Figure 13.1

Clarify Failure Unmistakably

Once you've clarified success, it might seem strange or redundant to suggest that you should also clarify failure, but it is equally important if you want the distinction between failure and success to be clear. Intellectually, most people will affirm the idea that failure is simply anything other than success; but in practice, the starkness of this assertion is off-putting. It seems so non-negotiable, and it highlights the fact that there are always many more opportunities to fail than to succeed.

Figure 13.2

So people tend to redefine failure or blur the lines a little to ease their discomfort and mitigate the threat of experiencing it. Conceptually, they make the boundary between success and failure less of a sharp line and adopt a definition of failure that is less encompassing than "anything other than success."

Most people fear failure, and I am convinced that this fear, and the unconscious line-blurring to manage it, is the reason so many leaders fail to give their teams clear finish lines. They see the value of clarifying success, but they instinctively recognize that the same degree of definition that will make success unmistakable for everyone will make failure unmistakable as well. That feels threatening, so they unconsciously dilute their definitions and leave the line vague, believing this will limit their chances of failure.

Figure 13.3

Unfortunately, that's not how it works. In fact, if you wimp out on defining failure, then you actually increase your chances of experiencing it. A diluted definition of failure always damages the definition of success, and when success is not clearly defined, it is rarely achieved.

If you try to make the distinction between success and failure more negotiable, you will find yourself recasting failures as "nice tries" and "near-misses," and you will soon be presiding over good efforts instead of true victories. This isn't leadership as much as it is marketing, packaging defeat for more comfortable consumption. Effective leadership is about cultivating a posture for progress by distinguishing success from failure and drawing a clear finish line. This isn't always comfortable for you or your team, but if you are going to keep their fire burning, then you will need to feel the heat, too.

Eliminate Limbo

The truth is, humans don't like failure, and they do whatever they can to avoid the prospect of it. They will even invent an unnamed and imaginary third option for performance that is neither success nor failure. I call it Limbo. It defies logic and description when revealed, but it is powerful in the subconscious and familiar to most of us. It's also your biggest adversary when trying to create a clear finish line for your team.

I first recognized Limbo in conversations with my honors students. When I informed them that they did not achieve an expected outcome on an assignment, they would often acknowledge that they did not succeed. But if I then asked them if they had failed, they would say "no" and offer an explanation. It was as if these two assessments were unrelated, or the qualifications for success and failure were not mutually exclusive. As I probed a bit deeper, I discovered that the students weren't consciously trying to outmaneuver me; they were genuinely reflecting their own mental model. In their minds, there was a sort of unconsidered and unexplored territory *between* success and failure, a third option for

Figure 13.4

performance that allowed them not to succeed yet not to fail.

Since that time, I've looked for Limbo in the assessments of creatives, executives, students, business leaders, and government officials. And I've found it present across the board. It's a prevalent coping mechanism that permits people to recognize when they do not succeed but also not to register it as a failure. This might protect an individual's self-esteem, but it is problematic for your team because it flips the polarity of performance. It allows the goal to shift quietly from being successful to simply not failing. Limbo becomes satisfactory, and Limbo is much too big a target to be a finish line at all. The teams and individuals that entertain it eventually find themselves living in it and leaving their highest aspirations unaccomplished.

In the end, Limbo is a fiction we've created to soothe our aversion to failure. Success and failure remain the only real options in performance. There is no middle ground. If you want your team to burn brightly, then you need to make this dichotomy clear and let them feel the heat.

This doesn't doom you to being a judgmental or hyper-critical leader. You can clarify the definition of failure starkly and still calibrate your responses to it, because failures aren't created equal. Some are debilitating or dangerous, and they deserve an assertive response. Others are relatively inconsequential and merit little response at all. If your goal was to produce a two-minute video and you produce one that is two minutes and thirteen seconds long, then it's a failure. But it may not be a big one if other things can be changed to accommodate it. It may not even be cause for concern, but it is still a failure simply because it did not achieve the criteria for success. Not every failure is the end of the world, and if it feels like it is, creatives will shut down; so calibrating your response is important.

Think of it this way. You want the *distinction* between success and failure to be like a light switch. It's either on or off. There are no other options. But you want your *response* to failure to be like a dial, adjustable and calibrated. It runs from 1 (a modest acknowledgement and nothing more) to 10 (a stop-the-world moment). You can turn it up and down appropriately. Be prepared to turn that dial often, because when you

184 | Dr. Andrew Johnston

make success concrete, clarify failure, and eliminate Limbo, you will see failures more often. You will also see better performance and real progress, because the finish line is clear and the heat is on.

chapter fourteen

Critique:

Tuning Up Your Timing, Truth, and Tact

Criticism, like rain, should be gentle enough to nourish a man's growth without destroying his roots.

—Frank A. Clark

EACH SEMESTER, I ask my graduate students what skills or practices they need to improve in their leadership. And every term, "Giving Constructive Criticism" is in the top responses. This tells me two things: 1) Critique is an integral part of leading people to excellence, and 2) Good critique is hard to find.

There's no doubt that critique is an important part of a leader's repertoire. Few things can turn up the heat on the quality and performance of a team like good critique. It affirms high aspirations, tempers and polishes ideas, and keeps everyone on track when the path ahead is unclear. Critique is like a signal fire that guides creatives to the place they want to be. Ed Catmull, co-founder of Pixar, observes:

> People who take on complicated creative projects become lost at some point in the process. It is the nature of things—In order to create, you

must internalize and almost *become* the project for a while… Where once a movie writer/director had perspective, he or she loses it. Where once he or she could see a forest, now there are only trees.[11]

If good critique is so important, then why isn't it more common? I don't think the problem is a lack of things to say. In my experience, most leaders nurture a sort of healthy discontent with the world that prepares them to critique it at any time. They're usually stocked with opinions to spare, but it can be a painful and unproductive experience sharing them with creatives.

Creatives are famously motivated from within, and this intrinsic orientation leads them to take their work very personally. Creating is not just a job; it's an expression of who they are. So they often take critique of it personally, as well. This can result in some difficult and emotionally charged conversations that tempt even veteran leaders to keep their critique to themselves. I think good critique is hard to find because it's difficult to give and difficult to receive. Intellectually, we know it's good for us. Practically, it seems too tricky or too painful to get it right, so we alternate between critique that is either ineffective or insufficient. That's no way to turn up the heat on people or projects.

If you want to kindle and keep the fire burning in your team, you have to give them good critique. The trick is to turn up the heat without making the creatives feel burned. This makes the experience more pleasurable and profitable for everyone involved. Here are some tips to improve your critique and fire up your team.

Make Critique Commonplace

When critique feels like a moment of reckoning in the midst of other things, it seems too conspicuous. It feels like an arbitrary or predatory interruption and puts creatives off. However, when critique is applied consistently and woven into the culture of a team, it feels natural and it's easier for creatives to receive it and profit from it. Everyone experiences it and it elevates the standard of excellence, empowers individuals, and enlists the vision and expertise of the entire team. Unfortunately, when your time and attention are scarce, it's hard to be consistent with making sure everyone experiences critique. It seems expedient to aim your critique at the lagging performances and lesser performers because the top performers seem to be doing well enough without it. This might save you a little time, but rationing your critique this way unleashes a negative version of natural selection that will ruin your team.

No news is always bad news to the top performers on your team, because they feel a sense of ownership for what they're doing and are hungry for your feedback. In the absence of it, their personal concern easily turns into self-doubt, and they begin to question both their contributions and your regard. This makes the feedback-free experience especially uncomfortable for them, and they are likely to go looking for a better experience someplace else. As these top performers leave your team, their roles are likely to be filled by less-invested people who find the feedback-free environment more appealing. In time, this will shift the composition of your team in the wrong direction until it is eventually filled with slackers. It is counterintuitive, but if you confine your critique to your least productive or lowest performing people, you'll only get more of them in the end.

To avoid this devolution, provide feedback to everyone. Make critique a common part of the culture, allowing everyone to experience it so that it doesn't feel odd or unwelcome.

An architect I know has accomplished this in fine fashion. His firm's offices are housed in an old church, and he transformed the odd-shaped room beneath the steeple into a sort of shrine to critique. He covered the walls with bulletin boards, added a couple of large video monitors, and named the space the "Crit Pit." Designers regularly post their work there, and the rest of the team is invited to offer critique. Project managers haul their clients into The Pit to explore options and debate. Creative teams hold standup meetings there to test and temper their ideas. The Crit Pit is a physical space that anchors a philosophical commitment. It elevates critique to a prominent and permanent position in the firm's culture that demystifies and destigmatizes it.

———

If you confine your critique to your *least* productive or *lowest* performing people, you'll only get *more of them* in the end.

Their team members worry less about getting burned by critique because it is part of their process and feels more like mutual problem-solving than evaluation.

Time Critique Carefully

Even when you've established an abiding commitment to critique, it is important to time it well in the creative process. Creating and critiquing are like breathing and eating, both vital to the health of your team but difficult and dangerous to do simultaneously. Creating involves broadening the possibilities, blurring the lines, and suspending the rules. Critiquing involves narrowing the focus, reasserting the lines, and reapplying the rules. You need both, but if you try to do them at the same time, you'll choke and neither will happen very well. Either creativity will dull the refining effect of critique, or, more likely, critique will shut down creativity. Timing makes all the difference.

Few things are more harmful to creativity or more frustrating to creatives than premature critique. It's like pouring cold water on their fire just as it gets going. You've probably been there yourself. You have the beginnings of a great idea and have just started to rough out the trajectory that will take it to something fantastic when your boss checks in to see how it's going. You barely start to describe the promise of the idea before she's nit-picking little details of its implementation or rejecting the shade of blue you used to sketch it on the whiteboard! It's not simply frustrating that she can't appreciate the potential of what you're describing. It's maddening that she is identifying all the things you already know will need to be done *before* there's been any opportunity to do them. It makes you sorry you even shared your idea.

If leaders offer critique too early, too strenuously, or too unexpectedly, their teams become preoccupied with anticipating problems and preempting their concerns. Team members start worrying more about hedging their bets and staying in the "safe zone" than trying new things or venturing out. This can quickly transform your adventurous team of creatives into a buttoned-down bunch of economists and editors. (My apologies to the rare creative economists or editors out there.)

It also causes team members to solicit feedback as late in the process as possible. This causes other problems, as leaders find themselves questioning or critiquing directions that were determined long ago, and creatives are too wedded to their choices to easily entertain alternatives. The struggle that ensues harms the product, slows the process, and frustrates leaders and creatives alike. Critique is most effective when it happens throughout the creative process, but one size does not fit all. It's important to tailor your critique to the time it is given, if you want creatives to receive it well or seek it out more often.

Next time you're giving feedback, take stock of where it falls in the process. Is the project closer to ninety percent done or thirty percent done? If it's ninety percent done, it's time to take off the kid gloves and nit-pick. The next stop is production or the public, so you need to correct anything that still needs correcting. Even the smallest details and incidentals are fair game and need to be addressed at this point. But if the project is only thirty percent done, this kind of granular attention is debilitating. It discourages creatives and takes the joy out of creating.

At thirty percent, projects are *supposed* to be incomplete and unpolished, because great things always start out imperfect. There's still plenty of time for the details to be addressed, so you should resist the urge to sweat the small stuff and offer broader ideas about where the project should be headed or reflect on the options that might be entertained. This gives you a chance to dream with your team members and offer thoughts they can consider or reject. This is what real collaboration and mutual problem solving feels like, and it's more enjoyable and profitable for both of you. Encourage thirty percent feedback as often as possible, and as your creatives learn that you can shape your feedback appropriately, they'll stop thinking of reviews like big reveals, and seek critique earlier and more frequently in their process.

Include Affirmation in Critique

Your team will also seek your critique more frequently if you do not limit it to negative observations and corrections. This particular kind of feedback is called "critique" because it is the result of *critical* thinking, not simply an abiding desire to *criticize*. This means that it should reflect a comprehensive understanding and provide affirmation and encouragement as well as correction.

It's easy to neglect the positive things. Even when your heart is in the right place, your schedule may not be, and you might be tempted to pare out the positives when time is tight. But this creates a negative bias in your critique that diminishes the enthusiasm and motivation of the people who receive it. It will put out their fire even as it turns up the heat.

Creatives enjoy the work of creating, and they are motivated by the opportunity to do it. But a steady diet of negativity will beat them up and wear them down. The unrelenting heat of it creates the kind of fear that is especially harmful to intrinsic motivation, and it will burn them out instead of firing them up. It makes them feel like the personal investments they are making aren't recognized or appreciated, and it's hard for their joy and initiative to continue in the culture of evaluation that results. So, when you turn up the heat, meter it with affirmation. Identify the good choices and positive points you see and include kudos in your critique when they are merited. Be as specific in describing the successes as you are in describing the problems so creatives can rely on your complete and unbiased review. This kind of affirmation not only encourages the recipients, but it also highlights positive principles they should repeat or reinterpret in the future.

Commit to Truth & Tact

In situations where the message you need to convey with your critique is not positive or affirming, it's especially important to pitch it right. If you're too pointed or come in too hot, you'll raise defensiveness and inoculate creatives against the very reflection or revision you're trying to promote. On the other hand, if you're too mealy-mouthed and dance around the issue, you'll lose the point and priority altogether. The best critique models a commitment to both truth and tact.

Telling the truth is important in critique because it's the foundation for your influence. When your team members know you are more committed to truth than to comfort in your relationship with them, they can trust what you have to say and open themselves more genuinely to your critique. Uncomfortable messages are the truest tests of this commitment. If you soft-peddle or water down the hard stuff, your team members may not fight with you, but they won't trust you, either. Your relationship with them will look good on the surface but will be weak or distant underneath, and this frailty tends to show up at the worst times. Few people enjoy being corrected by a leader, but when it's merited and doesn't come, they lose confidence in the leader's commitment to the mission and themselves. As a result, they bank the flames that are burning in them and draw back instead of stepping forward. They limit their openness and investment instead of upping the ante. So don't flinch from the heat in your critique; tell the truth, especially when it's a hard or uncomfortable one to tell.

But remember there are many ways to tell the truth. As a leader, your success depends on the efforts of your team members. How you exert your influence is ultimately secondary to how they respond to it. Put more simply, the real test of your leadership is not what you say as much as what your team does as a result of it. This means that if you want your creatives to truly digest and act on your critique, you'd be wise to make it as appetizing as possible. I am always surprised at leaders who rebel against this reality. It's as if they believe the truth is somehow truer when served as starkly and rough-edged as possible. Truth is truth, and it makes sense to serve it in a way that is easiest for the receiver to hear and digest, especially when it's hard.

When you need to turn up the heat, choose your time and tone. Pick your words carefully, not just for how they match the message in your head, but for how they might land best for the person who needs to hear them. You might be accurate and even eloquent in expressing your thoughts, but if you pay no attention to who needs to hear them, you'll find yourself raising defenses and creating resistance more than causing reflection or redirection. Tact is the leader's art of making a point without making an enemy. Don't dismiss others' perspectives or contradict their choices if you don't need to. Instead, add new ones, or try to bend the existing ones in a more productive direction. This isn't the same as diluting your message or being wishy-washy about your point. It's about "tuning" the message to the ears of the person you want to hear it to give it the best chance of getting through the other noise.

Let me reassure you, being strategic and intentional like this is not the same as being manipulative. Manipulation occurs when you are disingenuous and over manage the message. It's deceptive and often boomerangs on you, because it conveys a lack of confidence in both the judgment of your people and the truth you are trying to communicate.

The popular "sandwich" method for delivering negative feedback is a prime example of manipulation It's a recipe for critique that encourages you to say something positive before and after anything negative, and it sounds good on the surface. Bracketing an uncomfortable message with more pleasant ones promises to ease the recipient smoothly in and out of the hard stuff. However, in practice, this technique often comes across as artless and insincere and conveys a lack of respect to the recipient. It's not the best model for your team.

Creatives are characteristically sensitive, but they're not fragile, and they don't want to be treated as if they are. They want to be respected, not "handled", and a diet of these "sandwiches" makes them feel manipulated and devalued. Over time, this recipe reduces positive feedback to a decorative role in your interactions, and people start brushing it aside and bracing themselves for whatever comes next. You're better off building relationships where both positive and negative feedback are common, genuine, and able to stand on their own. Commit to truth and tact in your critique and save the sandwiches for lunch.

Ultimately, few things are as powerful as critique when it comes to turning up the heat on creative quality and performance. Unfortunately, some leaders think bringing the heat is simply about putting team members on the "hot seat" and making them sweat. That's pretty painful and unproductive for everyone, and creatives end up feeling burned instead of fired up. When critique is done well and integrated into your team's culture, it warms people to their tasks and to each other. It supports the creative process and deepens the relationships of the people participating in it. With all of that riding on it, it's worth the time and effort to get it right. Fire up your team by making your critique commonplace, timing it wisely, including affirmation, and telling the truth with tact.

chapter fifteen

Direction:

Focusing Collaboration with Purpose, Particulars, and Priorities

You have brains in your head. You have feet in your shoes. You can steer yourself in any direction you choose. You're on your own, and you know what you know. And you are the guy who'll decide where to go.

—Dr. Seuss

WHEN I LIVED in east Tennessee, I got a kick out of how people gave directions. It was a rural area where everyone knew each other and each other's business for generations. As a result, they took certain knowledge for granted and used a sort of community-based short hand when they gave directions. For example, if you asked how to get to the restaurant by the lake, a person might tell you, "Go down old 11 until you get to where the Clayton boy had his accident. Turn there. Take that a ways past the creek and look for the blue sign (or sometimes they park the tractor there) and if you get to the tobacco shed that burnt down last fall, you went too far." If you were an outsider or unfamiliar with the area, you were in big trouble. You'd be lucky to find the lake, let alone the restaurant! You needed clearer direction to get where you wanted to go.

In my experience, leaders often take certain knowledge for granted, too. They communicate with their teams, but they fail to give the kind of information their people need most and then wonder how they can lose their way. Sometimes this is because they confuse motivation or critique with Clear Direction. All three are important, but they are not the same thing. Let me clarify.

MOTIVATION IS ABOUT *SPURRING* ACTION. It's an important skill for you to have because your team members need some pushing and prodding to reach their goals, but spurring action is not the same thing as directing it. For example, if someone tossed a hand grenade into the room during your next staff meeting, it would surely spur some action. You'd see an immediate and impassioned response and an impressive increase in activity as people jumped out of their chairs and ran for the door, raced to far end of the room, or dove under the table. There would be a frantic scramble in every direction away from the grenade. That's motivation, but it's not direction.

Motivation gets people to move, but clear direction gets them to do it in a concerted fashion. It promotes collaboration and creates synergistic, focused effort. Leaders who miss this distinction rev their people up and spur them to action, but not necessarily to progress. They think they're directing their teams when they're just lobbing grenades.

CRITIQUE IS ABOUT *CORRECTING* ACTION. It's an important part of your repertoire, too, because individual and team contributions need to be tweaked and improved now and then. But correcting action is not the same as directing it, either. It may move people and alter their activity, but it does this inefficiently and discouragingly because it occurs so late in the game. That's the limitation of critique. It imposes expectations *after* action has already been taken, after the decisions have been made, and it creates more work and frustration than if these things were clear from the start.

Some leaders confuse critique with direction and practice a sort of "bumper car" leadership that is always trying to nudge people and projects into the places they should have been to begin with. This frustrates people in general and creatives in particular. You've probably experienced it yourself. A leader gives you only a vague idea of what you're to do, and when you deliver the finished product, he tries zealously to critique it into something else that he had in mind all along. You probably found yourself thinking, "Well, if you'd told me that's what you wanted in the first place, I'd have done it all differently..."

Motivation and critique are important, but when you want to fire up your team, they are pale substitutes for Clear Direction. They create and correct activity, but they are not enough to get your team to the destination you have in mind. In fact, if you're spending most of your time motivating or critiquing your team, there's a good chance your real problem is a lack of clear direction.

CLEAR DIRECTION *FOCUSES* ACTION instead of spurring or correcting it. It doesn't just turn up the heat; it aims the heat at one spot. Like a magnifying glass consolidating sunlight, Clear Direction collects the talents and capacities of individual team members and focuses them on a precise target. It fires them up, reduces their frustration, and enables them to move together toward the goal because it provides information missing in motivation and critique. It clarifies the Purpose, Particulars, and Priorities people need to know to get where they want to be.

Clear Direction

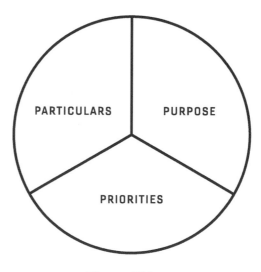

Figure 15.1

If you're spending most of your time motivating or critiquing your team, there's a good chance your real problem is a *lack of clear direction.*

Purpose

As a leader, you usually have a head start on your team. You've had time to mull things over in your own mind before engaging them in the process. During this time, your thoughts have likely moved from the big picture to the nitty-gritty, from your initial strategic impressions to the more operational details of execution. Now, when the time has come to give direction to your team, this makes it tempting to dive right into the What and How of the project without ever confronting the Why behind it. After all, time is tight and you're eager to get down to the nuts and bolts of the work to be done. That instinct to get specific is a good one. It will serve you well, and I'll encourage it in the next section. But it's premature at the start. So, resist the urge to dive headlong into the little things with your team before you've connected them to something bigger. Start with the Purpose.

Clear Direction begins with Purpose because when you provide creatives with a reason for their actions, you prepare them to think for themselves. This is vital if you want your team to stay on track or keep going when the going gets tough and unexpected challenges arise. It's impossible to anticipate every pothole in the path to success, and if you fail to clarify the Purpose for the work, your team will run smoothly only until it hits the first unexpected barrier or bump in the road. Then it will stall and wait for more direction from you.

This is fatiguing because you can't be attentive enough to keep everything moving, and it's frustrating because your team doesn't seem to be able to think for itself. The truth is, it is able; it's just not equipped. Think of it this way: if you want your people to reason, then you need to give them a reason.

Clear Direction creates coordinated effort, not by producing automatons, but by preparing team members to think for themselves in concert with each other. That's why the real quality of your direction isn't revealed when it's given as much as in the twists and turns of the time between setting the goal and achieving it. In this space, when the heat is on and things don't go as planned, unexpected challenges and complications change the equation, derail progress, and test the team's commitment to see things through. If members don't understand the purpose of the journey, they can only rely on the direction they received at the start, and when the anticipated paths are blocked, they will stop or wander off independently. But, if they have a compelling and common purpose, they can think for themselves and negotiate new routes instead. They can overcome the obstacles and remain unified as they take alternative paths toward the original destination.

Emphasizing Purpose in your direction is also the best way to raise the standard of excellence for the project. It's the merits of the purpose that ultimately justify the hard work and high standards you're expecting of your team, so this is the time to preach. You can really

Dr. Andrew Johnston | 207

bring the heat, because showing your own passion for the Purpose warms your people to the task and boosts the commitment and satisfaction of the team. It's a powerful investment in quality because it clarifies that the work is really worth it.

By contrast, if you neglect Purpose in giving direction, you don't have much to preach about. You are likely to find yourself strenuously nagging about less significant things to guarantee quality and passion when you're pushing about details, tasks, and execution is a different experience altogether. Lacking the foundation of a worthy purpose, it feels overbearing and nitpicky and becomes the kind of micromanagement that can quickly smother the fire in creatives. Pump up the Purpose to keep it burning bright.

Particulars

As important as Purpose is to clear direction, it is not sufficient. Creatives need more than the big picture to burn well; they need Particulars. If you fail to provide them, you create the same kind of no-win situation for your team that you've dreaded from clients and leaders yourself. That daunting proposition of, "I don't know what I want, but if you give me something, I'll tell you if you've got it right." For creatives, this is a set-up that promises only hard work and emotional investment without achieving the goal or satisfying the leader. If you want something specific in the end, then you need to ask for it up front. If you only hit the highlights, you'll be frustrated when your team doesn't produce what you wanted, and you'll frustrate them in return by clarifying it after they've worked hard to deliver something else. A lack of Particulars also diffuses the imagination and talent of your team by failing to aim it effectively. Clear Direction is supposed to focus the capacity of a team and equip creatives for *concerted* effort. This means that it names the targets and drives out any misperceptions or diverse interpretations that might leave people pulling in different directions. It gets everyone on the same page by describing essentials like What by When, Givens & No Go's, and Riddles & Results.

1. What by When

At the very least, the Particulars in your direction should identify the deliverables and the deadlines. Your people need to know what needs to be done and when it needs to be done if they are going to successfully achieve the goals. More importantly, each contributor needs to understand these expectations in exactly the same way. This means that you will need to be as specific and concrete as possible. When there is fog or vagueness in the Particulars, your direction is not clear and will cause confusion down the road.

An old Saturday Night Live skit illustrated this in a humorous fashion. In it, the foreman of a nuclear power plant gives a pointed warning to his team as he leaves the facility, "Remember, you can never add too much water to a nuclear reactor." His team nods knowingly, but after his departure, the water level alarm sounds and they start arguing about what he meant. Did he mean that it is bad to put too much water into the reactor, or that you should add plenty of water because no amount is too much?

In your case, you may not be tempting nuclear disaster with your direction, but there is always fallout when you fail to describe deliverables and deadlines to your team in unmistakable terms. Don't let negotiable terms go undefined in your discussion of Particulars; operationalize them. Make interpretation not only unnecessary, but impossible. Consider these examples:

- "We need some ideas quick." (Ineffective)

- "We need some good ideas next week." (Better)

- "We need the team to pitch its top 3 ideas on Wednesday at 2:00." (Even better)

- "I need a video bumper for next week." (Ineffective)

- "I need a cool video bumper for Thursday's run-through." (Better)

- "I need a fast-paced, pump-'em-up video bumper less than 1:30 for Thursday's run-through." (Even better)

2. Givens & No-Go's

When you communicate clearly about deliverables and deadlines, you are clarifying your expectations for the *product* of your team's efforts, but your team also needs to know your expectations for the *process* of their work. Sometimes the route is as important as the destination. For this reason, it is helpful to identify any givens or "no-go's" at the start so that people know how to efficiently spend their efforts on the way.

Givens are things that *must be* included in the process. They may be particular aspects of the deliverables, individual steps in the process, specific people to include in the process, etc. "No-go's" are things that *must not be* included, such as resources that cannot be used, people who should not be engaged, processes that cannot be employed, etc. When you are giving direction, you should make any givens and no-go's clear so that the team can honor these parameters as they move forward. Here are some examples:

- "We'll need the venue production team to be on board, so make sure you pull one of their members into the planning team." (Given)

- "Let's use some of the materials left over from the project last month." (Given)

- "That guy is busy and going another direction, so don't rely on him for this project." (No-Go)

- "We're outta time, so skip the mock-up meeting."
  (No-Go)

- "The client is going to photocopy the final logo,
  so the design can't be too detailed and needs to
  work in black and white as well as color." (No-Go
  and Given)

As a general rule, if you will consider any specific aspects of the process in your evaluation of people's performance when the job is finished, you should communicate these things when it starts as Givens or No-go's. This makes your expectations clear and not only safeguards your preferences, but also provides a richer road map of the route to success.

3. Riddles & Results

Of course, if you don't want to create automatons, there is a balance to be struck in providing the Particulars. You need to nail down enough of the details to give clarity and protect the team from wasting its energy and imagination on unproductive directions, but you also need to leave enough loose ends to spur creativity and energize creatives' sense of initiative and control.

Think of the Particulars as framing an engaging riddle for the team. "How do you accomplish this result, by this deadline, with these givens?" In the riddle, you have the opportunity to elevate or protect the things you care about most, but you're also not dictating every little move. You're simply outlining the space in which the team will play. These boundaries guide creatives toward success and protect them from wasted effort and disappointing results. They also clarify where creatives can exercise their own discretion and authority and where they cannot. If you pose the riddle well, your team will trust you and appreciate both the boundaries and the space they provide. As they grow more confident that their energy and effort will be well spent, they will be inclined to give them generously as well.

Independently, Purpose and Particulars are insufficient to take your team to its destination. Providing Particulars without Purpose smothers creativity and leaves creatives busy and bored. Preaching about Purpose without giving any Particulars suckers creatives and gives them a high bar with no idea of how to clear it. But together, Purpose and Particulars are a potent combination. They are a powerful one-two punch that links behavior to aspiration and prepares your team to do the right things.

Unfortunately, in the whirlwind of organizational activity there are too many "right" things to choose from, and its easy for creatives to spread themselves too thinly or struggle to decide what's most important. That's why you also need to establish Priorities in your direction.

Priorities

Priorities help people spend their energy and attention strategically by clarifying what matters most. Historically, the word "priority" was superlative and singular. It meant "the most important thing," but sometime around the industrial revolution, people started pluralizing the word. Life was becoming more complex, and they needed multiple "priorities" to order it effectively. Today, the complexity of life is downright overwhelming, and it's almost nonsensical how we use the word "priority." We keep long lists of the most important things, but when a list gets this long, it begs the definition of "most important." The practice seems more of an effort to ease our consciences than to actually elevate anything in our lives above the rest. There are simply too many items on our lists, and the old adage proves painfully true. "When everything is a priority, nothing is."

Ironically, it is often this abundance of priorities in an organization, not the scarcity of them, that leaves people confused and unproductive. In their book *The 4 Disciplines of Execution*, Chris McChesney and Sean Covey paint the impact of too many priorities in vivid terms.[12]

Their data indicate that having too many priorities actually makes a team less productive. In fact, if you attempt to elevate more than three things above the whirlwind of the other things that keep your operation running, you harm your team's ability to achieve any of them.

Number of Goals *(In addition to the whirlwind)*	Number of Goals Achieved
2-3	2-3
4-10	1-2
11-20	0

Figure from *The 4 Disciplines of Execution.* © Chris McChesney and Sean Covey.

Figure 15.2

Unfortunately, effort and attention are finite resources. When they are spread too thinly, there is not enough allocated to anything to get traction or to make a difference. The abundance of priorities leaves people spinning in a whirlwind of important things and dilutes attention until nothing is achieved. Clear Direction safeguards productivity by telling people which priorities are most important and focusing attention on a precious few.

In my experience, being this brutal about prioritization is tough. It's not too difficult to distinguish Important Things from the unimportant ones, but it is downright painful to elevate the Most Important Things above the important ones. When I ask leaders to identify their priorities, they have little trouble making lists; but when I ask them to number the items on their lists in order of importance, they struggle. It's surprisingly difficult to prioritize a list of things you have already identified as priorities, but that's exactly the kind of choices that matter most in the messiness of real life where our priorities contend with each other for a share of our talent and attention.

It seems we are always facing an impossible choice between two or more genuinely important things. To make these choices, we don't simply need to know what's important to us hypothetically or in a vacuum; we need to know what's *most* important to us relative to the other things we value. If this isn't clear to us, we are not making those choices. We're just playing games and convincing ourselves that we are prioritizing things when we are not.

In practice, elevating a few priorities above the rest takes courage because it rarely feels like you are preferring those few as much as you are betraying all the rest. This can make you retreat from preferring anything and content yourself with juggling all the things on your list instead of advancing any of them. That's not going to get you or your team where you want to go. Clear direction identifies priorities, but also gives guidance on what to prefer when the priorities contend with each other. It elevates the Most Important Things above the merely important and prepares your team to recognize and reconcile the tension when their values collide. Following are some examples:

- "I'm not sure the Director will be thrilled with this strategy, but we're going to press for it." (A particular strategy prioritized over the approval of a key person)

- "We need to find a way to accomplish it without additional funding." (Frugality prioritized over impact)

- "I want something beautiful that we can be proud of even if it we need to cut back on the number of features." (Quality over breadth).

In the end, giving Clear Direction is one of the greatest investments you can make in your team's success. This seems almost too rudimentary to mention, yet most leaders fail to do it. They are eager to start the journey and skimp on the details up front or they take certain understanding for granted and wonder why their teams get lost. Clear Direction takes more time and attention than you might think, but it's worth it because it prepares your people to allocate theirs more effectively. It enables them to be more productive and collaborative and to require you to provide less motivation and critique. You won't need to work as hard to keep creatives' fire burning because your effort to clarify the Purpose, Particulars, and Priorities focuses their flames and lets them turn up the heat for themselves.

chapter sixteen

Risk:

Embracing the Inseparable Nature of Success & Failure

Fortune sides with him who dares.

—Virgil

EVERY NOW AND then, I hear an enthusiastic leader declare, "Failure is not an option!" and I cringe. He's honed the steely-eyed stare and set his jaw, or she's squared her shoulders and is listening to the inspirational music rising in her head, but they're both headed for trouble. Failure is an option any time you dare to do great things, because it's integrally connected to success. If you minimize or marginalize it, you're not turning up the heat on your team. Instead, you're reducing the risk, and the fire in their bellies will go out. Firing up creatives is more about maintaining the risk and managing the relationship between success and failure.

In my experience, most people misunderstand the relationship between success and failure, or they recognize only a poetic correlation that makes for a good story after success has been achieved. For example:

- Thomas Edison failed 10,000 times before he succeeded in creating a commercial light bulb.

- Walt Disney was fired from the Kansas City Star paper because he "lacked imagination and had no good ideas."

- Winston Churchill failed the sixth grade and lost every election for public office prior to becoming the British Prime Minister at age 62.

- Steven Spielberg was rejected from the USC School of Theater, Film, and Television three times.

I appreciate the hope or encouragement these examples provide, but there is a more important and practical relationship between success and failure than these kinds of stories suggest. Leaders of creatives need to appreciate the inseparable and proportional nature of it if they want to fire up their teams.

Success & Failure are Inseparable

Failure isn't a popular topic, so we don't talk about it much and tend to oversimplify it. Conceptually, we cast it simply as the opposite of success and imagine that the two exist at opposite ends of the same continuum.

FAILURE ⟵⟶ SUCCESS

Figure 16.1

Unfortunately, this perception is inaccurate and can lead you literally in the wrong direction. If failure and success were truly on opposite ends of the same continuum, you would not need to pursue success in order to achieve it. You could simply avoid failure and eventually back your way to victory. I realize it sounds silly to say it this way, but that's the opportunity this picture suggests. You could consistently recoil from every risky situation, anything that's not a sure thing, and ultimately find yourself successful.

Intuitively you know that doesn't work. In real life, playing not to lose is different from playing to win, and the difference revolves around risk. When you play not to lose, the main objective is to minimize risk. You work hard to avoid the prospect of failure and hope you will back your way to victory. Unfortunately, you can play it extra safe and hedge all your bets and still miss the payday you were hoping for. If you avoid all possibility of failure or loss, you won't wind up successful; you'll wind up safe, unremarkable, and unfulfilled. In the tight economy of success and failure, you never win bigger than you bet, because there is simply no risk-free route to success. You've got to go big, or go home.

Given this, it's more accurate to think of success and failure as existing at the same end of the continuum with Mediocrity at the other. This better represents the inseparable nature of the two, and the hard truth that any effort to back away will only distance you from the other and leave you in the bland between.

MEDIOCRITY ←————→ SUCCESS/FAILURE

Figure 16.2

This picture may not seem like a grand revelation, but it can make a big difference in your leadership. As a leader, you act out your inner dispositions instinctively throughout the day, often without conscious thought or reflection. You frequently set directions and priorities for your team without even recognizing that you are making choices. For this reason, the way you conceptualize things matters. It shapes your actions and decisions more than you realize. If you picture success and failure simply as opposites, you may not recognize that you are distancing your team from success when you are minimizing its prospect of failure. So, adjusting your mental picture to represent the inseparable nature of success and failure recalibrates your inner compass and redirects the choices you make for your team.

Success & Failure are Proportional

As you refine your understanding of the relationship between Success and Failure, consider that they are not only inseparable, but they are also proportional. This means that they are correlated and that you can never pursue a success that is larger than the failure you are willing to risk. If you want a big success, you must risk a big failure. If you're willing to risk only a small failure, you can only hope for a small success. There are no magic calipers to measure such things, but you know the difference.

Some accomplishments are relatively small, like a good review or a great parking place. They make you happy if they happen, but you don't live off that satisfaction for very long. They risk only small failures—like a worse review or a longer walk—that you can shrug off with little lasting impact. Other successes are bona fide Big Deals, like a major business investment or an important relationship. If they work out, they make you more than passingly happy, and they get tangled up with your identity in a good way that makes you feel more capable, more you. The failures these successes tempt are Big Deals, too, like bankruptcy and break-ups. These are the kinds of failures that can put a dent in you and mess you up for a while.

The point is, if you want to lead well and prepare your team to feel the heat of high aspirations, then you need to embrace both the inseparable and proportional relationship between success and failure. You need to recognize that winning can only exist when losing is an option, and that the trophy you will raise is only as substantial as the loss you might suffer. In other words, you can't enjoy a meaningful success without risking a meaningful failure, and you can't protect yourself or your team from the kind of failure that hurts if you want to experience the kind of success that makes you proud.

This recognition has important practical implications. If you miss this correlation, you'll set inspiring goals but end up presiding over only mediocre achievements. You'll start out well enough, with good intentions and lofty aspirations, but then you'll start hedging your bets. You're not trying to downgrade the success you've targeted; you're just trying to minimize the risks you need to face in pursuit of it. In the moment, this doesn't feel like you're settling for less or wimping out. It feels responsible and prudent, like you are wisely protecting yourself and your team, but this kind of safety comes at a cost.

Diminishing the size of the failure you are risking always dials back the size of the success you are chasing. It turns down some of the heat, but it also causes you to back away from the success/failure end of the continuum altogether and lower the bar without realizing it. When this happens, you and your team will still accomplish things, but lesser things, and not the ones that fired you up in the first place. This phenomenon is quiet and invisible, but it is prevalent and powerful, too. It's the reason many promising leaders and initiatives wind up "successful" but unremarkable in the end.

Once you recognize the inseparable and proportional relationship between success and failure, you understand that keeping the heat on your team is largely about embracing and managing the risk that accompanies extraordinary results. Here are some tips for doing that well and firing up your team.

Manage the Likelihood of Failure
Instead of the Magnitude

It's not decreasing the *likelihood* of failure that damages success; it's decreasing the *magnitude* of it. Likelihood is about the possibility of a failure occurring. Magnitude is about the impact of it when it does. Think of the difference like this: If you are a rock climber, it makes sense for you to protect yourself by taking every precaution and exploiting every piece of equipment to minimize your chance of falling as you climb to the top of a spectacular cliff. Those strategies manage the *likelihood* of failure, and they're just plain smart. It's a very different, and ludicrous, strategy for you to protect yourself by climbing only to the top of an eight-foot ladder instead. That strategy would manage the *magnitude* of failure. It protects you, but it changes the whole scenario and damages the success you'll celebrate in the end. The pride and exhilaration you feel when you climb to the top of that cliff is precisely correlated to the dizzying drop at your feet. If that drop is inconsequential, then your sense of accomplishment will be, too. That's probably why you see so few selfies and GoPro videos shot from the peaks of eight-foot ladders.

To keep your team fired up, you need to safeguard their success. Don't let your efforts to protect them from failure diminish their accomplishment in the end. Work to decrease the likelihood not the magnitude of failure. Anticipate the things that might derail a project and plan for them, but attack the threats themselves instead of changing the project to eliminate the possibility of them.

For instance, if a stakeholder thinks your goal is too ambitious, don't change the goal; change the stakeholder. Don't avoid the threat; take it on and persuade the individual to share your point of view. Changing the goal might protect the team from failure, but at the expense of its aspirations. Changing the person, however, protects the team while safeguarding the sense of accomplishment it hopes for in the end.

Recognize the Risks of Innovation

The opportunity to do new things is a big factor in keeping the creative fire burning in your team, but innovation is also risky. When you step out from the things that are tried and true, you might be starting the next trend, or you could perish quietly in obscurity. You won't know which one will happen until you try, and this risk keeps many people close to what they've seen and done before. You can see this principle played out in the demise of network television and the rise of cable and streaming services.

For many years, network television programming lacked originality because studios didn't want to risk their resources on uncertain bets. They protected themselves from failure by greenlighting only the new projects that looked like previous successes. Executives didn't want to risk their jobs on their ability to recognize the "next big thing," so they hedged their bets and nudged new productions to look as much like the *last* big things as possible. Their notes to directors, driven by this fear of failure, pushed derivative and uninspired content and primetime programming devolved into a featureless expanse of CSI clones and reality competitions.

As streaming and online services stepped into the arena of original content, they bet big on originality and innovation, and they won big. They distinguished themselves by taking the creative risks networks were avoiding and they urged producers and directors to step boldly into new visions instead of revamping old ones. The freedom and support they provided spawned a revolution in the format and a new golden age of television. If you want to win big with your creatives, you need to embrace the risks that come with creating. Accept that innovation is never safe and that some promising ideas won't pan out. Celebrate originality even when it goes awry. Demonstrate the courage it takes to step off the well-worn path and support your team when it chases the next big thing.

Protect the Dreaming from the Doing

One of the best things you can do to support your team is to keep the risks inherent in chasing the next big thing from shutting down their ability to imagine it.

When was the last time someone on your team pitched an idea that frightened you or made you think: "That's exciting, but impossible," or "Yeah, that would be great, but there's no way we can pull it off"? If you can't remember the last time this happened, there's a good chance your team is managing its prospects of failure too carefully. It's not embracing the risk and its fire is starting to ebb.

When creative teams are fired up, they dream big. They push the envelope creatively and propose some pretty crazy stuff. It's natural to feel some doubts or concern about the execution of it now and then, because the most innovative or inspiring ideas are rarely the safest bets or easiest wins. Part of you is always weighing the feasibility of their ideas and calculating what it will take to make them real. As a result, it's tempting to let the challenges of the doing creep into the dreaming, and to adjust the ideas to be more realistic or doable even as they are being generated.

This seems like a good move because it could prevent the team from wasting time discussing less doable options. Unfortunately, this isn't as helpful as it seems. It might redeem some time spent on futile forays, but it also keeps many ideas from coming up at all. It quenches the spark of innovation.

If you want your team to stay fired up, you need to embrace the risks of dreaming big and keep your concerns about feasibility to yourself, at least for a while. Trying to minimize failure during the process of identifying success will wind up giving you only a modest amount of each. Instead, let the discussion run and delay any talk of the doing until the dreaming is over. Let imaginations soar recklessly and consider any compromises the execution of them will require after the team has arrived at a vision they can burn for. This will keep creatives dreaming and keep them from managing their risks at the expense of their aspirations.

Recast Failure as Your Friend

If Failure lies at the same end of the continuum as Success, then it is prerequisite to the things you want the most, and you need to make sure your team won't back away from it. So, recast failure as your friend and demonstrate that you are comfortable with it in the mix. Successful creatives and creative teams court failure constantly because they know it is an inseparable part of the creative process. They know that exploring new ideas or applications inevitably leads them to some dead ends, but it also leads them to happy accidents, inspirations, and destinations they could not have discovered by any other routes. For this reason, failure comes up often in discussion but doesn't suck the air out of the room or quench the fire in the team.

Have you failed enough recently to assure you that your team is being truly creative? If you can't recall any failures, then you're either hedging your bets too much, or you are uncomfortable calling anything a failure. The best teams identify failures but don't wither in the face of them. They treat them like mile markers and fail forward on their journey. Keep track of the most important failures you encounter and take the time to celebrate how they've contributed to your success. This may test your own perspective and creativity as a leader, but it will powerfully reframe failure in the eyes of your team. It will demonstrate that you're paying attention and that you know a failure when you see it. More importantly, it will tell creatives that you welcome failure because it affirms that you are aiming at the right end of the continuum and that mediocrity is not an option.

Don't punish mistakes

Since failure is ultimately your friend, you need to be careful not to cast it as the enemy. Be mindful of how you respond to your team's mistakes and missteps, because your behavior in the midst of the work will communicate your disposition toward failure more powerfully than anything you say in meetings and memos. Try not to hold on too tightly or turn up the heat on the wrong things. You want to be attentive to the things that might diminish the quality of work or the credibility of the team, but you don't want to turn mistakes into "Public Enemy #1" because perfectionism is counterproductive. It marginalizes the risk inherent in creativity and draws creatives toward the safer but mediocre end of the continuum. In that case, they will try to avoid mistakes at all costs, and their work will become increasingly perfect but pedestrian.

This doesn't mean that you should pretend not to see mistakes, but take extra care to cultivate the right attitude with your response to them. Don't turn up the heat in ways that make creatives feel burned. Ask creatives to fix their mistakes, but don't rub their noses in them or penalize them for their performance. If you embarrass or shame them for missteps in the service of good goals, they will stop stepping altogether. Instead, craft your response to model resilience and the right posture toward risk. If a capable team member drops the ball on an important project, you will make a bolder statement to your team by assigning the next big project to him than you will by putting him in the "penalty box" for a month.

Recurrent mistakes are a different matter. They represent a failure to learn and merit an assertive response, but be careful to identify the trend rather than the immediate incident as your concern so that the message to your team stays clear.

Over all, when it comes to embracing risk and firing up your team, the takeaway isn't simply, "The more risk, the better." That's just plain recklessness, and sooner or later you and your team will get burned. It's also not simply that you should pursue bigger successes and tempt greater failures in general. That's an assessment you'll need to make. Risk is relative and depends on the situation.

The point is to revise your mental model to recognize that the correlation between success and failure is non-negotiable. If you are only willing to tolerate a small failure, there's no shame in it, but don't fool or frustrate yourself or your team by expecting to achieve a big success as a result. There's no bargaining without consequence, no something for nothing. You've got to pay to play, and you and your team will only enjoy returns commensurate with the prospect of loss. If you want the kind of success that breathes life into you, be prepared to risk the kind of failure that sucks it out of you. You've got to brave the heat that comes with lofty goals. Creating is exhilarating in part because it is never safe, so go big or go home.

Endnotes

1. Ed Catmull and Amy Wallace, *Creativity, Inc.: Overcoming the Unseen Forces That Stand in the Way of True Inspiration*, (New York, Random House, 2014), Page 90.

2. Kathleen D. Ryan, Daniel K. Oestreich, *Driving Fear out of the Workplace: Creating the High-Trust, High-Performance Organization* (San Francisco: Jossey-Bass Inc., 1998).

3. Stuart Brown "Let the Children Play (Some More)" https://opinionator.blogs.nytimes.com/2009/09/02/let-the-children-play-some-more/ (Sept 2, 2009)

4. "New Discoveries in Psychoneuroimmunology" an interview with Dr. Lee Berk, Humor & Health Letter, Humor & Health Letter, vol 3, no. 6, 1994.

5. Bill Burke/The Travel Guy "Explaining a delay, Virgin style" http://www.bostonherald.com/entertainment/travel/the_travel_guy/2013/03/explaining_a_delay_virgin_styleMonday (March 11, 2013)

6. Charles Duhigg, "What Google Learned From Its Quest to Build the Perfect Team" http://www.nytimes.com/2016/02/28/magazine/what-google-learned-from-its-quest-to-build-the-perfect-team.html (February 25, 2016)

7. David Sloan Wilson, "When the Strong Outbreed the Weak: An Interview with William Muir," https://evolution-institute.org, (July 11, 2016).

8. Evan Polman, Kyle J. Emich, "Decisions for Others Are More Creative Than Decisions for the Self," http://journals.sagepub.com (February 11, 2011).

9. Viktor E. Frankl, *Man's Search for Meaning*, (Boston, Beacon Press, 1959), page 75

10. Mihaly Csikszentmihalyi, *Flow: The Psychology of Optimal Experience* (Harper Perennial Modern Classics, 2008)

11. Ed Catmull and Amy Wallace, *Creativity, Inc.: Overcoming the Unseen Forces That Stand in the Way of True Inspiration*, (New York, Random House, 2014), Page 91.

12. Chris McChesney, Sean Covey, and Jim Huling, *The 4 Disciplines of Execution: Achieving Your Wildly Important Goals*, (Free Press, April 24, 2012).

About The Author

Dr. Andrew J. Johnston has made a life of leading teams and developing the people within them. From Bridgestone to Walgreens, the YMCA to the U.S. Army, the Center for Non-Profit Leadership to the Christian Leadership Alliance, countless organizations and brands have turned to Johnston to teach, coach, and consult their teams to new levels of success.

For over fifteen years, Dr. Johnston developed and directed Belmont University as Associate Provost & Dean of Students, and he continues to advance education as a member of the graduate faculty at Vanderbilt University.

Combining his degrees in Interpersonal Communication, Counseling, and Leadership, along with his experience as an executive leader, Dr. Johnston connects personally and powerfully with other leaders and their teams. He knows what it takes to lead well, and continues to emerge as a leading voice in organizational and leadership development.

Looking for additional resources? SALT wants to equip and inspire you to reach your creative potential. Our free resources were created to help you with you daily workload. We offer everything from lyric templates to event planning checklists, design program shortcuts to filmmaker resources, and much more! Head over to SALTcommunity.com/free-resources to download all these amazing and helpful resources!

Made in the USA
Middletown, DE
26 April 2019